Making the Cut

By Kasonde Bowa

ISBN 9982-07-491-1

Cover photo: Kasonde Bowa

Copyright Kasonde Bowa 2011

All rights reserved. No part can be reproduced or copied in any form or media –graphic, electronic or manual- without written permission

Published by   Kasonde Bowa and Partners

This book is dedicated to young people everywhere, with the belief that they will meet the intellectual challenges of their time and be able to carve for themselves a future far better than the one we leave to them. This is the challenge that one generation must give to the one that follows it.

I also dedicate it to my parents who helped me become what I am today. My wife Theresa who is such a delight, my son Wandi who never ceases to amaze me, my daughters Chiku and Chesu who are both such great treasures.

But most of all, to God who makes something out of us when we are nothing at all.

I also wish to acknowledge with thanks the help of the team at the Curriculum Development Unit of the Ministry of Education who helped me to bring the book up to a standard suitable for Senior Secondary School reading.

Table of Contents

1. Foreward..	6
2 Preface..	9
3 Genesis..	11
4 Growing up..	12
5 Preschool..	16
6 Early School years...	20
7 Munali Secondary School..	31
8 Boarding School..	36
9 Lessons Learnt..	38
10. University...	42
11. UNZASU Strike...	46
12 Lessons learnt from Medical School...............................	68
13 Final year	74
14. Internship...	76
15. Getting Married...	87
16 University of Glasgow..	90
17. Marshlands...	101
18 Ireland Game Changer..	118
19 UNZA School of Medicine...	131
20 Epilogue...	133
21 Glossary..	148
22. Photo..	153

Foreword

Professor Bowa struggled to put pen to paper (or fingers to keyboard) in order to write his autobiography for us to read. Understandably, we all do not want to be thought of as simply wanting to blow our own trumpets. There is something repugnant about that and it causes us no small discomfort when we think of such an undertaking.

However, having known this man from the time he first set foot onto the University of Zambia as a teenager, to the present day, I would have no hesitation in commending him for breaking through his natural reserve and giving us this wonderful living story. Those of us who know Professor Bowa will be the first to say that he rarely—if ever—talks about himself and his achievements. I have been his pastor for over a quarter of a century and most of these achievements have only come to my attention in this book!

Every generation needs to rise higher than the generation before it. This can only happen if each generation has some idea of the great feats of its predecessors. Sadly, we have very, very few biographies to help the younger generation know what the current "record" is so that they can aim higher. That is what Professor Bowa has done for us here. He has set a benchmark for those whose shadows are currently darkening the doors of our educational institutions. As he himself asks, "Will they make the cut?"

Something that can easily be missed in this book because it has not been stated is the need for balance in order to achieve long-lasting success. Although Professor Bowa does not make much of this, having watched him over the years, I think that it was also the balance he sought to maintain between his spiritual and social, his physical and domestic, and his academic and career lives, that explains his success. Being his pastor, I can say for sure that his faith in Christ has played no small role in making him what he is today. I hope that those who read this autobiography will read between the lines and notice this balance. Too many people fail to reach his heights because they concentrate on one aspect and neglect the rest until it is too late.

Having finished reading the book, I would want to put it into the hands of all teenagers and young adults who are starting the journey of their tertiary education and careers. They need to see the price that must be paid for success and the pleasure of being single-eyed. Too many young people are jacks-of-all-trades and thus remain masters of none. They think that it is lucky chance that brings their buddies to great heights. This book will smoke such notions out of their brains. Rather, it echoes the poem that says,

**"Heights, by great men reached and kept,
Were not attained by sudden flight;
But they, while their companions slept,
Were toiling up through the night."**

Professor Bowa is still in the morning of his career. Seen from my vantage point, he is still a young man (though from the vantage point of the younger generation that needs to read this book, he is getting on in years). Hence, my prayer for him is that as his sun rises, may it continue to do so and never set until God calls him to his final rest. May those who will succeed him, those who will write the second half of his life, prove that although what is recorded in these pages is inspiring, by the grace of God, it was but a foundation of an even more inspiring life that followed after this.

Pastor Conrad Mbewe

Senior Pastor Kabwata Baptist Church

B.MEng(UNZA),M.Phil

Preface

I have decided to write an autobiography. Initially I thought myself arrogant to do it. I asked myself several questions. Are there not other people whose biographies deserve to be written? Those who have achieved more in life, in politics or in medicine. First I hesitated then I answered myself. Sure there are greater men then I, men or women with better stories to tell who are better known. But some have no interest in writing no aptitude for it and though they may have achieved greatness, perhaps their path to it was mundane. I have both a love for writing and what to me is an interesting story to tell. If this be presumption then I am guilty of being presumptuous. The mere challenge to write my story well has spurred me to try it. Will any one read the biography. Well perhaps no one will. Even if that is the case I will at least have succeeded to recount my story the way I saw it. Perhaps my children or friends or grandchildren will pick it up and read it. Maybe they may glean something about life, happiness, ambition and love. Perhaps they will do better than I have done. I certainly hope so. Whether this work is printed or not or it remains in manuscript form only. I'll at least be glad for the challenge to have tried it.

In writing this biography I make one disclaimer, the truth has many faces. This biography represents the face I have chosen. Other people may not see this history with the same eye that I do. I will accept their right to do so, as much as I hope they will accept my right to do the same. Like everybody else there were things at which I was good and others in which I was not so good. I hope I have presented myself with sufficient balance to be neither seen by those who may read this book as a villain or a hero. I hope that the story will strike every one as believable and true. What I can say is that I have enjoyed writing my story and I hope those who read it will enjoy it as much as I have enjoyed writing it.

In my life I have made many friends, I hope I have made no enemies. Most certainly I may have made some enemies. I hope that this biography will make me more friends and reconcile to me those who may have not cared much for my manner. I hope it will make someone smile and perhaps make someone laugh. If it does this even for one person perhaps then I will consider it to have been well worth it. I dedicate this work to those like myself who have always tried to do their best and to work hard to help those who they meet along the journey of life. I hope they will learn, as I have, that happiness in life comes mainly from making other people happy especially the young. I trust this story will make young people happy and give them hope about the future.

When my wife read through the draft she suggested that I should write the story in such a way that it would also be a motivational book for young people everywhere. This I thought was a good idea, so I reworked the book with that goal in mind. So, I have tried not only to share my life but also my heart with the reader. I hope I have succeeded. I will leave you to be the judge of that.

Kasonde Bowa
Ndola, Zambia

GENESIS

When the name "Kasonde Bowa" from Zambia was announced by Professor Edward R Laws the President of the American College of Surgeons at the Morial Convention Centre in New Orleans Louisiana USA it had a distinctly foreign ring to it. It wasn't one of the names commonly heard in gatherings of this type. I stood up graciously and took the customary bow. My face showing on the myriads of TV screens in the plenary session room. It was a great honor for a young boy born in the remote African town of Kawama in Mwense district in Luapula province in Zambia. A place, which is unknown, to many living in Zambia itself, let alone in the United States of America. In that flash of a second my whole life run through my mind up to that point. The story of my childhood, growing up in Kitwe in Copperbelt province, going to secondary school at Munali, the University Of Zambia School of medicine, getting married, becoming a Doctor and studying in England the whole experience of life. It was a mixed story with scattered episodes of sorrow and happiness. With triumphant moments, and some less triumphant moments. It was an interesting story nonetheless. I decided then that it was a story worth telling. In the three months that I had taken leave from my post at the University of Zambia School of Medicine in Lusaka to come to the United States, perhaps I could start to write my story. I had been awarded by the American College of Surgeons the internationally competitive award, called the International Guest Scholar for the year 2004. It was the first time this award had been given to a Zambian doctor. I dug deep into what was left of my literary talent if any to write my story. It has taken me over 8 years to complete. The French Physician Andre Breton once wrote "Of all the arts in which the wise excel, natures chief master piece is the ability to write well". If I have not achieved this, at least it can be said that I tried.

∙∙∙

GROWING UP

My exact date of birth is uncertain, though I am very sure of my year of birth. My date of birth often vacillated between April and February and was to my amusement a source of quarrels between my mum and Dad. My father was a teacher and sometime in 1965 he had been transferred to teach in a remote village town of Kawama in Mwense district in Luapula province. While my mum and dad where working in Kawama I was born. Probably in February, or perhaps in April. My father could not recall precisely nor do I that of my children. It is a typical male indifference one might say, but one that is very common in Africa. The men finance the home and the women take care of the details. My mother had seven children and mixed up the birth dates of several of them, which is probably understandable.

I choose when I was older since it proved to be of some importance to others, to have been born on the 13th February 1965. Which I later learnt was a Saturday. The date proved mischievous later when it turned out to be related to some western superstitious belief. Something of which, I was oblivious of at the time. Had I known perhaps I would have chosen the more neutral date of the 16th April. In those days birthdays were treated with an indifference that would be very strange to many of our children now.

My recollection of my early childhood is very basic and lacks in much detail. My father was a teacher professionally; his name was Christopher Chisala Bowa. He was commonly called CC. He was a tall sensitive man with a sound intellect. I learnt later, that he was taken to be a good looking man. Some old photos show this to have been the case. He was the Head Master of Kawama primary school in Mansa in Luapula province. Mansa was and is still the provincial capital of Luapula province. My mother Judith Nsomi Bowa was a petite beautiful woman with a rather sharp tongue. She was Chisinga or Ushi both dialects of the Bemba language, Bembas make up over 40% of the Zambian population. Their women were renowned for a rather sharp tongue. She used this with ruthless efficiency both in and outside the home. Very few people were courageous enough to get onto her wrong side including my Dad. She had a quick intellect and made it clear she had underachieved by marrying my dad. Her brother our maternal uncle had the unusual distinction of being one of the first Zambian graduates. In those days it was the same thing as been rich .I learnt later that he had studied for a Bachelor of Arts in Economics at the University of Makerere in Uganda. His intellect was the thing of legends, my mum made sure we were aware of this fact. My father in contrast was a shy demure man bore my mum's frustration and tongue with what I can only be called, a great level of fortitude and dignity. The home was surrounded by a great deal of martial disharmony. Which some may dispute, but about which I myself had no delusions. In spite of this the memories of my childhood were happy ones. I had four brothers and two sisters, this made for, quite a rowdy home. In those days in the 60s and 70s this was the norm. We shared what we had, fought and generally had a good time. My parents were not rich by the standard of the time, but at the time the key export, copper, was fetching a good price on the London stock exchange. The country was wealthy. Prices were good and we had a decent, what one might call a middle class life style. My father who had a flair for politics and business had a grocery store in his home village of Chipili, just outside Mansa. My brothers, and I the three eldest boys, attended a private school in Mansa called Mutende primary school.

My mother was a teacher at the local primary school in home economics. Luapula province is one of 9 administrative units of Zambia. The division has increased to include Muchinga province since 2011. So that there are now 10 provinces.Luapula provinces is one of the largest of these provinces.The Zambian map looks like a preschool attempt at drawing a butterfly with one wing smaller than the other. A strip of Congo DRC juts greedily into Zambia and creates this unshapely appearance. This being some of what remains of the history of the scramble for Africa in general and Zambia in particular represents the Belgian King, Leopold 2's attempts at getting some of the lucrative copper spoils on the Copperbelt province in Zambia. Katanga province of Congo DRC dips ungraciously into Zambia producing the C or butterfly appearance. The Luapula province which bears the brunt of this intrusion shares a large border with Congo DR, part of which is occupied by the Luapula River which runs a course between the two countries. Historically the Bemba had emerged out of the Congo and invaded the local tribes in the area. The main language now spoken is Bemba although several dialects persist in the area. My father, too, prided himself in being Bemba and insisted that his folks had migrated from the Bemba kingdom to work and settle in the Anglican mission in Chipili, which is just outside Mansa. He laid claim to royalty from his maternal Grandmother. My mother also claimed royalty from the local Chief Mutipulas line. This apparently trivial matter, to me at any rate, was the source of conflict in the home. My mother who was Chisinga from the Ushi people, who were indigenous to the area, had her village, Mutipula very near the Chipili mission settlement. My maternal uncle was apparently in line for succession to Chief Mutipulas' throne. This struggle for the dominance of the Ushis and Bembas was frequent in the home. My mum with her quick tongue and volatile temper was keen to show that my father's claim to the Bemba royalty was presumptuous and exaggerated. He on the other hand was keen to show the validity and reasonableness of these claims. In these arguments' he stood more firm than he did in others. The Anglican settlements in Chipili had a great influence on my father and therefore on the family. He had been educated by missionaries from the Anglican Church in Mpanza in Choma in Southern province of Zambia.He unlike my mother was a devote Anglican. I learnt from him that at my christening the Anglican Bishop of Southern Africa, of the time, had given me his name "Oliver".This apparently was a great honor. It was also made clear to me that I was only one of 2 children bestowed this honor. The other was Trevor Oliver Mwamba, who became an Anglican Priest himself and subsequently rose to become the Anglican Archbishop of Botswana. It is a name though which I have attempted to erase over the years with limited success. Not because I'm oblivious of the great honor that it represented, but simply because the more I grew older the more I learnt the assertiveness that comes from being native. This leaning has become increasingly common among many Africans. In part because so much that is negative has been directed towards Africa. In rallying to the defense of Africa the easiest thing for many of us has been to give eminence to African names. My mother named me Kaunda, which was the name of her mum. She said frequently that my maternal grandmother had expressed the frustrations of being born in a gender imbalanced time. She said that she would like to have had a chance to be a man. Many African animist beliefs were strong on reincarnation and believed in inheritance of the spirit of the dead. This was effected by naming of the new born .This revealed the sometimes contradictory approach to religion my mother had. In all fairness, though, so did many of her peers of the time. She was a practicing Christian, but incorporated many African animist beliefs without seeing the obvious contradictions. So we grow up under the heavy influence of education, tradition and Christianity. My father was a perceptive man for his time. He knew very well that future success lay in being well educated. He pursued this himself and gave it the utmost priority among all his children.

We lived in Mansa up to 1971. In 1971, the family moved to Kitwe the second largest city in the Copperbelt Province of Zambia.

PRESCHOOL YEARS

My recollection of these years which were spent in Mansa is poor. Nonetheless some interesting memories linger .Two things stand out in my mind in those years. The first is my own recollection; the other is from the stories doing their family rounds. It was said that when I was hungry, this is a source of mirth in the extended family for a generation; I was given to temper tantrums. In addition, during these period, I would start screaming and hollowing " Ubwali, Ubwali"(which means nshima, nshima- the local maize meal which is the staple food in most of Zambia) while threatening to walk to my paternal grandmothers house in Chipili. Perhaps this is why I have never really liked Nshima. I find it to be rather bland and lacking in imagination as a food. It is commonly eaten in Sub-Saharan African in different forms and varieties. One English man described it aptly, as a tasteless maize meal cake, which the locals swear by.

I was a happy child but I suffered constantly from pain in the testis. Something which is ironic because I would latter spend a lot of time as a Urologist treating children and boys with this very problem.

These episode came as severe attacks, during these periods I'd come screaming out of the house "ka ingila ka ingila" (it has disappeared it has disappeared). The claim was that my "Willy" (private parts) was disappearing into the tummy, and this was the cause of my pain. I recall being taken to a big hospital in the city to be examined by a doctor for this problem. It became so severe that at some point a group of women from the village were brought in to provide some traditional treatment to resolve this problem. I ended up with several tattoos around my waist with the symptoms subsequently disappearing. I'm not quite sure which of the two treatments provided the cure. I was only too happy to see that this severe problem disappeared as I got older.

Thinking about it years later, I concluded the hospital to have been, what is now called the Maina Soko Military hospital in Woodlands

Lusaka. It was a private nursing home at the time. In the 1970s' President Kaunda, the first president of Zambia, abolished all private health services, in order to provide equity in the health service provision. The merit of this decision is still debated by some.

The tattoo marks represented the attempts to secure my fertility from interfering sprits that roamed the Africa villages to deprive innocent young boys of their future seed, and more seriously, bored elderly women of chubby grandchildren, this rather than the formers was most surely the concern of the Banafimbusa(Elderly Women Counselors) who worked their craft on my unsuspecting waist.

My father had the habit of taking us to his home village at Chipili mission about once a year. It was not more than 100kms outside Mansa; we would also proceed on to my mum's village in Mutipula which was not more the 10kms outside Chipili. The road was not tarred and the journey was rugged. There was also no electricity at the time, though now the electricity grid has reached the mission. My mother's village had an even smaller road with a small and unsteady bridge, which flooded from time to time. The Chipili mission, had been established by the Anglicans 100years earlier. The village had developed around the activities of the mission.There was a school, a church obviously and a hospital. Many people of prominence have come out of the Chipili area, some of whom were the Mfulas,Mr Jason Mfula was MP and deputy speaker of parliament, the Matipas, Mr Andrew Matipa became an Ambassador to the UK, I think, the Mwambas, of whom I had spoken earlier, whoes son became Archbishop of Botswana,the Lufungulos, the Lumbwes, Dr Brigadier General Chishimba Lumbwe, became Physician to the 3rd President of Zambia,Levy Mwanawasa and others whom my father was proud to list on the WHOs' WHO of Chipili mission. Some interesting names of places around this area which were a source of amusement to me and my brothers were Kwa Mutwe Wa Nkoko (literally the place of the Head of a Chicken), Kwa Mukoma Nsala(literally the place where they dig the hunger) and Kwa Kabunda fyela(where equipment has been drowned).They were two big rivers in the vicinity tributaries of the Luapula no doubt, the Mutipula and the Chipili streams.

On one of these occasions we visited my mum's village, where my Dad ran a small grocery store across from the river in the centre of the village. I had taken my tricycle and was playing happily along the main dusty walk way of the centre of the village. Suddenly a woman appeared running for all she was worth and screaming on the top of her voice "Kafwimbe Paul na putula, Kafwimbe Paul na putula" meaning literally Kamfwimbe the son of Paul is loose. Now apparently there was a mad man in the village who was a danger to the community and was always chained to a tree trunk in his father's compound. From time to time when his insanity reached its peak he would uproot the tree and reign havoc on the village. This was one of those times. All the villagers, who were less naïve then I was, emptied the walk way rapidly. I only, 4 years old, was less so. When I moved my eyes with bemusement from the scampering distraught female fleeing in the distance, they came to rest upon a burly huge man hovering menacingly over me. He held a huge tree trunk the size of a small hut over his shoulders. His eyes met mine and they were as calm as the Mutipula River. I wondered why he was carrying this heavy trunk over his shoulder and was about to venture to ask him so. Before I could, I found myself tackled to the ground and whisked to the safety of a nearby hut, by an agile kindly elderly woman. We were shut into her hut for what seemed an eternity and the door heavily barricaded.

When I was recovered by my parents, recriminations followed and appropriate gratitude was given to the brave elderly women. I off course oblivious of my recent escape could not determine what the fuss was about. However when we went back to search for my tricycle and found it strewn on the walk way, I realized my parents could have been scraping me off the walk way with a spoon if it hadn't been for the brave elderly woman. With hindsight I concluded that Paul Kafwimbi suffered Manic Depressive Psychosis, a form of mental illness that leads to severe mood swings, from extreme violent aggression to passive deep despondency. After this our visit to the village was less frequent.

Another experience I had was my visit to my paternal Grand fathers place in Chipili. My dad had built him a quasi modern house just off the main Chipili Mansa road, which was the envy of his mates. We found him often on the front pouch sipping the local brew from the Insupa. The insupa is an earthen pot with a snout that is used to store water and alcoholic beverages. The snout acts like a modern day straw. In the village, the elders, typically the men, sat around the fire each with his insupa, told stories and discussed the matters of the village. My Grandfather had the habit of calling us each by name and suffixing the name with the phrase "Chatile chobe", this meaning literally "your thing-your private part". So I would be summoned in this manner "Kasonde come here your thing or your private part". I half expected my Dad to reprimand his old man, being very strict on the use of coarse language as he was. However to my amusement, my dad explained this speech as a form of endearment, and not to be understood as an insult. It was the sort of guy thing, akin to the modern clapping of each other's shoulders that men may do in our times as a form of camaraderie. My paternal grandmother, a kindly elderly women, of royal descent according to my dad, on the other hand suffixed our names with "amalumbo" literally praises. The Bemba tradition of naming as in many cultures was premised on the belief that the spirits of the dead continued to live in the new born babies. Therefore they carried along the characters of the ancestors. So each name had the accolades of success of those ancestors that had borne that name in earlier generations. Two, which I recall where my name Kasonde- which would be followed by "uwa fisama muchimbusa, uwa cinfeya inkalamu" literally who has hidden in the bushes and a whole volume of poetic praises, including he who has struggled and defeated the lion. My elder brother was Chanda chikulula, uwa lenga a basenshi uknoka", literally he who has made the white people rich. These experiences enriched our growing up years in Mansa.

EARLY SCHOOL YEARS

We moved to Kitwe in 1971 from Mansa. It was the beginning of a new phase for me. I was six and recall arriving in Kitwe in the evening to the dazzling appearance of the bright lights of the city. We stayed in Parklands in a two bed roomed semidetached flat at Richmond gardens just adjacent to Freedom park, which was then one of the main community parks in the city. We were 4 children at the time, all boys, which in those days was seen to be a small family. My father had changed jobs from his last job as a headmaster to Personnel Manager at the Kitwe City Council. We had been transferred from the private school in Mansa to Fredrick Knapp School in the mining area of Nkana West. The school was later named Rokana primary school. The economy of Zambia was then as it still is heavily dependent on copper. Even then there was talk of diversification to agriculture, but I guess it was just talk. Kitwe was a busy bustling city far different from Mansa were we had lived before. The chief three mining towns were Kitwe, Chililabombwe and Chingola. Now, off course, Solwezi has emerged as the new giant mining town.There are various methods of mining copper depending on its location. Zambia had one of the largest open pit mines in the world in Nchanga in Chingola. The Nkana underground mine in Kitwe was one of the deepest mines in the world then. While Chililabombwe (which literally means the crying frog or toad), had the dubious distinction of having one of the wettest mines in the world.Perhaps this was why it had so many croaking toads!

Kitwe is the commercial centre of the copperbelt. Ndola is the administrative centre. This dichotomy (sharing) of functions was no doubt intended to spread development in a vast underdeveloped country. Kitwe city introduces itself characteristically to its visitors as the hub of the copperbelt. This was quite an apt description. My formative years were spent in Kitwe. Over the 7 years I lived in Kitwe I grew rather attached and fond of the town. It soon became clear that like my elder brother I had a knack for learning. By the kindness of fate I had a good sound reasoning power from my dad, a sharp intellect from mum and sufficient discipline to do what I was told by my teachers and to do it well. I have learnt over the years that of all of the things that nature gifts men with, discipline is by far the most important, it is the single most important determinant of success, and the one to be sought after of all other gifts, that nature gives to its children. For now I will leave it at that.

I started school at Rokana primary school in grade 1. My first few years in school was a blur. I could not make sense of anything well into grade 3. I realized I was doing well in school when my Dad bought me some toy cars for doing well in school. I was not really convinced of this but was happy to accept the toys. He took me to the large department store in the centre of town called ZCBC. I was completely taken by this, and decided that it was a wise idea to do well in school. I remember finding "sums" arithmetic very confusing. I was very pleased when in grade 3 it suddenly occurred to me that "times" or Multiplication, was simply a modification of "plus" or addition. It came to me as revelation when I realized that 2 times 2 simply mean 2 repeated 2 times. In about 1972 we moved to Kantanta Street in Kitwe central. By this time the family had grown to 6. We had two younger sisters.

Sometime in Grade 2 because of watching the black and white cowboy movies I had an accident. My young brother and I, had the habit of play acting cowboys and Indians. We did mock punches and mock fist fights. On this occasion just before class, we did a mock fist fight. In the process I slipped and hit my head against the edge of the bed. We did our cover up bit, as children do and innocuously got to school. While at school I started vomiting and became unconscious. When I came round, I found myself in the hospital. This I learnt latter was the Kitwe Central Hospital. It was an experience not easily forgotten. I stayed a couple of days and there was talk of an operation, which was eventually not done. It turned out I had an extra dural hematoma. This is bleeding between the coverings of the brain and the skull. It appeared to have been mild and had settled without requiring further treatment and surgery. The hospital was a thoroughly unpleasant place I found. It was scary at night, the nurses were fat and brush.

On several occasions I contemplated jumping from the window next to my bed, and escaping the intolerable prison. However It was somewhat high, and my nerve could not hold. I was fortunate to go home after what seemed an eternity. From that time on I had persistent and intolerable temporal headaches. My mum of course had several local remedies for this. This headache has stayed with me well into my 30s. It was a brief but unpleasant introduction into medicine that made me averse to medicine as a career. I'll pick up this thought later and explain how this mindset was reversed many years later.

My Dad drove a small Datsun 1200. He had the misfortune of having it stolen, while he was at a meeting at Edinburgh Hotel in Kitwe. It was a story my mother accepted with a heavy dose of skepticism. When this happened we reverted to walking to school, from number 11 Kanyanta Avenue to Rokana primary school in Nkana East. It was a 30 to 45 minutes walk. I was about 10 years old. By the time I was in grade 4, I remember my academic record was improving. I recall Mrs McGee our Canadian teacher had me moved from the third row to the second. In Grade 3 we were made to sit according to class performance with the best students in row 1. In 1975 we moved from Kitwe Central to Riverside on the other side of town. I was transferred to Valley View primary school in Riverside. We lived at 33 Zambezi way. Riverside is in the south east part of Kitwe town. It was a slightly more up market place with larger houses. When I was in Grade 5, I recall a girl in my class whom I liked, her name was Naomi Banda. I also recall my Grade 4 teacher whom I didn't like at all, his name was Lembani Peter Banda.

I changed schools for a third time to Valley View primary school. It was a good school and unusual in having only one class in each grade. This made teaching a little more personal. It was started by the community in the area and was therefore held in great affection by them. I moved in grade 5 and became aware for the first time of a competition in education. I came out as 10th in class. By grade six I was first in class.

My father was a part time referee in the football league. We therefore were able to watch for free a lot of the local matches at Buchi Stadium in Kitwe.I remember meeting with some of the key players of the time, Ucar Godfrey Chitalu and Kaiser Kalambo.We were all soccer fans in the family.I remember once at Dag Hammarskjold stadium as it was called then, in Ndola,meeting Kaiser Kalambo the national team player who played in defense at the time.His thigh was the size of a tree trunk. We joined the local football teams and played with other teams for money.This was interesting but occasionally resulted in fights over the monies.I was a fairly good football player and being left footed I played in the left wing position, which required speed and dexterity. By 1976 I was playing for the school team and remember scoring in some of the major competitions .One of my greatest triumphs was to score the winning goal from the left flank at the school match against the local team River Rain primary school. I was a local school hero for a few weeks. In grade six I was chosen a prefect, which was a great honor.

Increasingly I became more studious as I grew older, becoming more aware of girls and increasingly awkward around them. Growing up among a predominantly all boys home and inheriting a sensitive and shy nature from my father did not help matters at all. We had neighbors who were a largely boys group also, with a few grown up sisters. One of these girls was in my class. I felt a lot less awkward with her. I grew up with an amazing code of decency, never to swear or have any girl friends. This was unusual for a boy of my age at the time. The code worked well and carried me safely through secondary school when the male hormone surges run riot and caused all sorts of problems.

I was so shy and timid in class that I rarely spoke unless spoken to directly. It took the class teacher often quite a while to realize that I was actually one of the cleverest kids in class. It was a character failure which I would not encourage in any one, and one from which I suffered a great disadvantage in the later years of university and medical training. I found later that when you become part of a group of increasingly intelligent young people who are as clever, some cleverer, then reticence becomes a grave disadvantage.

About this time I became very good friends with a Indian class mate called Barhavin Acharya.I did not know it at the time but this influence would have a tremendous impact on my future life and career years later. He was a brilliant fellow, studious with a keen eye on the future which was common of Asian children of the time. His father was a science teacher at the local secondary school, Kitwe boys and he lived in Parklands not very far from where we lived.We developed a good and close friendship. He had a vast and encyclopedic knowledge of general science and math that were a wonder to me. I was always forced to read to just keep up with him. By this time in the late 1970s the economy of the country was beginning to falter, the copper prices were declining and the price of oil was increasing. The liberation wars of Zimbabwe, Mozambique and South Africa were having a telling toll on the country, which before then had, had excellent economic fortunes. The family's fortunes were declining with those of the country. The large family of now 7 children was a stress on my father's resources. We had lost the luxury of bicycles which we had enjoyed in the earlier years. There were no birth day parties; I don't recall having neither my own tooth brush nor many of my own underpants. We were reluctant to invite any friends home, because the house was crowded with lots of children and cousins staying with us.

I developed as a result two groups of friends. The school friends, who were the rather more elitist group from an upper social class, and my home friends who were the more rugged guys from the local communities with whom we played football over the holidays. I kept the two life styles quite distinct. During holidays I would avoid at all costs any of my school friends. Whereas my uniforms for school were all smart and great. My home clothes were somewhat less so.

I remember typically one day when my grade 6 teacher asked me to go and collect a bottle of milk from my house for a class demonstration, which she knew was no more than 5 minutes walk from the school. I was in a state of panic, because I knew pretty well there was no such luxury in our fridge. To my great relief my neighbors daughter Beatrice Mwando who was a rather cute but showy girl, given to being on centre stage offered to do it. It was a stage which in this case I was happy to let her take.There were many pretty girls in my class, some of whom I remember to this day.Some of whom I met later in university; one whom I recall was a girl called Chanda Mumbalanga.I never had the courage even to say hi. My cousins who were a bunch of rather rowdy women gave me the rather dishonorable term of "uku ungutilwa" which has the closest meaning in English of being a "dope". My favorite song was Kenny Rogers's song "The coward of the county" which kind of summed up nicely my demeanor at the time. It probably saved me from a lot of problems in the early years.

About this time I made friends with a boy called Chris Mutale, he lived one road behind our house. He was an avid reader of books though he was a poor football player. In those days football was everything, so he was largely ignored by everyone else. He was an exceptional boy with the unusual skill of speed reading. He consumed books at the rate that most boys of that age consume biscuits. Through him and my Dad I was introduced to the Kitwe public library and reluctantly, at first, began to read a lot of the story boys of the time, the series of children's stories by Enid Blyton, the famous five and the secret seven. Classics like Gullivers' travels and Treasure Island by Robert Louis Stevenson.I began to love reading so much that I determined that I would grow up to become a famous writer.

My faintest recollection of an interest in Medicine was in Grade 6 at Bahavin's 10th birthday. In those days birthday parties were not an everyday occurrence. There were the preserve of the upper classes. So to see one was rare enough, to be invited to one was rarer still. In spite of this it was a birthday I was embarrassed to attend. Two things concerned me, the first was what I would wear the second was what I would give as a birthday present. Worst of all I had no idea how one behaves at these types of events. I thought of every conceivable reason I could why I could not go, however to my chagrin, my friend was determined, that as his best friend, I should be there. Rather reluctantly I was compelled to attend. It turned out quite to my surprise to be a great deal of fun. Most of the people there where Bahavins family and were Asian. The focus of attention was on Bahavin, which as a shy young boy suited me very well.

I recall distinctly the cutting of the cake. Bahavins elder sister called him up front and said that since he was going to be a surgeon he must learn how to handle a knife. It sounded very fancy and caught my ear. Its meaning was lost to me, until many years later when fate forgot, mixed up the names and decided that I was the one to become the surgeon. Bahavin became a pilot in the USA. My progress in school was interesting, because I started grade 1 in 1971. So each year represented my grade of study. In 1977, I sat for my grade 7 examinations. This was at that time the transition period from primary school to secondary school. It was the first major filters of those who would be something and those who would not. This exam was a major challenge for children my age at the time. My immediate elder brother Mulenga had failed this exam the previous year. This created for me a sense of unease. My eldest brother Chanda had passed the exam very well many years prior to this. With my character of reclusiveness, I had developed a pessimism unusual in one of my age .I had a continued sense of impending doom, a morbid fear of the dark and of the future. So when exam time came I was afraid. I was about the best student in my class so the fear was at odds with the facts. My father had told me earlier that to be successful I had to be among the top five students in my class, and this had always been my target. However so great was my pessimism that I was sure that my exam papers would be lost and that I would fail.

In 1977 my Dad was transferred to Lusaka to work at Lusaka City Council from Kitwe City Council. We were allowed as it turned out to remain in the house we had been staying in for a further 3 months. It took Dad a while to settle in Lusaka and find a suitable house. It was also decided that since I was in an exam year I should remain with my mum and complete my examinations in Kitwe. This proved to be a distressful experience. The first major blow was that we were evicted from our house on 22 Zambezi Way riverside. The new tenant got impatient with the continued stay of the family and had us forcibly evicted. It was an experience I would rather not have had. My mum who at the best of times was explosive was livid. The new occupants found themselves on the wrong end of some very unpleasant language. However the man of the house was not deterred until we were finally evicted from the house. The council was kind enough to sense the potential embarrassment and moved us to a house in Lunsenfwa close on the other side of riverside. The house was smaller, and to my shock and surprise had no electricity. Some outstanding bill from the previous tenant meant electricity had been disconnected. I prepared for my grade 7 exams in this somewhat tumultuous environment, studying by candle light. I, also, now had to walk for almost 30minutes to get to school.

When the first examination paper was to be done, my mum who was somewhat superstitious gave me a handkerchief with salt, which she said would calm my nerves. In those days many people held the belief that to do well in class you needed to possess some magic. Many of my class mates believed that I used magic to do well in class. So when I appeared at the exam room with a hander kerchief, it attracted a lot of attention. Several of my class mates shared the salt which was prescribed by my mum that day.

With exams finished the family moved to Lusaka. Lusaka is the capital city of Zambia and the main commercial town. Even in 1977 it was a very different city from my home town of Kitwe. It had a larger population and was more cosmopolitan. We found also that we had to learn "Nyanza". This is a dialect of Chewe, which is spoken in Eastern province. It was very difficult at first and really did not make sense at all. Gradually I adapted and found that I conversed quite well in the language. Since my hospital experience in Grade 2, of having been admitted to Kitwe Central Hospital, I suffered unexplained pessimism. My fears of death and the dark had grown over the years as had my general pessimism about life. It appeared that my sense of doom and misfortune increased as I got older. My expectation was that my Grade 7 results would go missing and I would be said to have failed.

Fortunately this did not happen, however I kept my pessimism. When the results for grade 7 came out that year in 1978, I recall getting one of the best results in my class and perhaps in the province, I scored 733 marks. My Dad said I could go to any school I choose. I decided to go to Munali Secondary School. This I understood to be a famous school which produced the most educated people in Zambia. It is commonly said that John Mwanakatwe a previous Minister of Education and Dr Kenneth Kaunda studied at the school. It turned out though that I had to first attend Kitwe Boys Secondary School for a few weeks before being transferred to Lusaka. I learnt that having been selected there initially I could not go to any other school. So I returned to Kitwe with mixed feelings of pleasure and trepidation. Trepidation, because I would have to stay in Ndeke with my cousin, who was really regarded as my sister because she had grown up with the family since she was in primary school. My elder brother was in Form 5 at Kitwe Boys Secondary school and had stayed to write his examinations before moving with the rest of the family to Lusaka.

Kitwe Boys Secondary School proved to be a challenge in many ways. We were living on the periphery of the city in Ndeke Compound and the school was on the other side of the city towards Chingola road.We were required to be in class before 07:30. We had to wake up well before sun rise. Getting on to the buses in Ndeke that early after a cold bath was not the easiest of things for a 13 year old boy.It was a harsh introduction into secondary school, like the system of teaching, with several subjects merging rapidly into each other with different teachers was novel and stressful to the mind. I was just beginning to wrap my mind round the system when it was time to move to Lusaka again.

Going back to Lusaka to start school at Munali Secondary School was an adventure I had long looked forward to. However it proved to be a little more than I had bargained for. When I was told I would have to travel by bus from KMB(Kitwe Main Bus Stop) to Lusaka Luburma Market my stomach turned. It was not without go reason. I resisted this idea, but it was completely futile, there was no way of getting to Lusaka quickly enough to start school on time. There was also no one else to travel with. My elder sister took me to the bus stop, gave a generous tip to the conductor to take care of me in the big city and after all the niceties and what seemed like an eternity waiting for other passengers we started off for Lusaka. The buses were called Moyo buses and were notorious for break downs. We started off for Lusaka at about 15:00hrs, we finally arrived at 01:00 the following morning. The vehicle spluttered and coughed all the way from somewhere like Kabwe to Lusaka. We spent several hours off the bus with the conductor and driver frequently under the hood with oil smudges all over their clothes. With declining sunlight my feeling of fear about my journey and its ultimate end grew. I not only did not know Lusaka well, but I also had no idea about the towns in between. So I was never sure where we were or when we would arrive. The anxious faces of the other passengers were also not reassuring at all. The men in the bus also grew increasing drunk with each stop; they imbibed alcohol at each stop with reckless enthusiasm. This for all its disadvantages, at least somewhat lightened the sense of gloom in the bus. When we arrived I did not quite know it. The bus stopped at an abandoned large bus shelter in the centre of town. I was unsure what to do, but I was probably the only one. The bus emptied within minutes. I starred nervously out of the window with the hope of recognizing something or someone. The conductor graciously offered me a blanket and suggested I spend the night in the bus. It was quite safe he said. He pointed out that there were several security guards around the many large premises around the station. It's the safest place you can be he encouraged. Someone will come for you in the morning he said confidently. I glued myself to the seat and hurdled myself round the blanket he had generously given and prepared myself for a frightening night in this jungle of a city. Not too long after that I heard heavy footsteps in the aisle of the bus. When I looked up my Dad was smiling at me disarmingly as he often did at such times. Not too far behind was my benefactor, the conductor, who ensured he got all the credit for my safe though late arrival. My Dad was a quiet man he spoke softly but always with precision and an overbearing weight of logic. I always said if words were money, my Dad would have been a rich man many times over. He saved his words. He only said what needed to be said. On this instance he made an exception, his words were effusive. The emotion and anxiety of the events probably had something to do with it. He explained how he and the rest of the family had moved around all the key bus stops in Lusaka trying to locate this elusive Moyo bus for the last 4 hours. For my part I was only relieved to have been rescued from what I can only describe as a misadventure. Thus I was introduced to Lusaka and lived there for 33 years.

MUNALI SECONDARY SCHOOL

Munali Secondary School was a prestigious school. Many of the Zambian leaders in the post independence days had gone to Munali. So I was keenly aware of this when I entered the school in about February 1978. I found myself disadvantaged in two ways. Firstly having come in a little late at the school, it was commonly perceived that one had not earned their place. There was talk of corruption and patronage. My second disadvantage was that having come from a town other than Lusaka, my primary school was unknown, therefore it was generally expected that I would not measure up to the high standards of the school. I found in fact that the standards were not that high and I quite easily excelled, almost to the surprise of all my detractors.

My maternal Uncle was Mr Vincent Nsomi, a man it could be said at the time, of means and education. He was my mum's elder brother. He studied Economics at the University of Makerere in Uganda, at a time when most civil servants in Zambia had not gone beyond high school. He had excelled in his professional career. He was previous Post Master General and General Manager of ITT supersonic, which was later called Erickson's. It was a Swedish owned company of some renown at the time. He had been to Munali secondary school and was on first name basis with people like John Mwanakatwe, Elias Chipimo(Senior) the father of the current politically active leader of one of the political parties in Zambia, Vincent Mapoma, Francis Kaunda and several of the elite Munali trained people who managed the financial means of the country.His son Chibale was 2 years my senior at Munali so I often got a ride with them to and from school. He was a generous and ambitious man. I learnt in the course of my association with him, two things that proved important. He extolled the value of a career which allowed self employment. He regretted that Economics was not a good choice in that context. He stirred clear of the politics of the time and was skeptical of the prevalent distinctly socialist philosophy of those days. These two things allowed him to become financially very successful, well beyond many of his peers.

Within the first term of my stay at Munali I discovered that the school was quite elitist. Many of my class mates were the children of very highly placed parents in the political and financial corridors of power. None the less I became good friends with many of them. Some of my class mates were people like Patrick Chona (his father Mainza Chona was vice president or secretary general of UNIP), Mukozo Nkowani (whose father was governor of the bank of Zambia), Lubinda Lisulo (his father Mr Daniel Lisulo was also Prime Minister for a while) and several other distinguished people of the time.The school class lists read like WHOs WHO of Zambia. I settled in uneasily among many others of my friends who were of a more modest middle class upbringing. Within my first year of school at Munali I was one of the top students in my class. Some of my teachers took notice, and were curious to know which school I was from. One of them having not heard of Valley View Primary School, to my surprise, insisted that I was from Lusaka High School. Which I later learnt was a prestigious school with top grades in the town.

My father decided, in the middle of my first year that I should enter Boarding School. Living in Woodlands, made travelling to the school very difficult every morning. So before I knew it I was being hustled into May house at Munali Secondary boarding section. The school was an all boy's school with a mixed number of day scholars and boarders. A fact to which, I had been completely oblivious prior to this. My experience at boarding school was a little more than I had bargained for and I spent quite a few of my first weeks in sheer misery. Eventually I learnt to cope, and managed to get some benefit from the experience.

My first stressful experience occurred soon after I had been left at May house in the boarding premise of the school. May house was the fourth of a series of five double blocked dormitories for student residence. I learnt eventually that each house had an administrative structure from the house captain, house prefects and wing monitors. Each house had

2 blocks. Each block and two conjoint dormitory wings. Each wing in a dormitory contained up to 30 double bunker beds set up in rows with lockers in a military barrack style. This meant that up to 60 students could sleep in one wing; therefore each house had up to 240 students. The wings were arranged by form. So that form 1s occupied wing A, form 2s wing B and so on. The end of each wing had two single rooms which were occupied by the House Captain, his vice and the house prefects. The House captain and his team of prefects were selected by the staff each year from the Form 5 classes which were 4. The wings had two rows, at the end of each row of bunker beds was the wing monitors bed. He was in charge of supervising the students in his row. The wing monitor was selected by the house prefect in charge of that dormitory, from among the mature students who occupied the dorm. It was a distinct privilege to be a wing monitor. The wing monitors carried themselves with a great sense of accomplishment. They would probably have been equal to a lance corporal in the regular armed forces. They disciplined those under their charge with relish and frequency that was disheartening to watch.

It was like discovering a totally new life within the school system. I learnt quickly that understanding this rather unwieldy system of bureaucratic student management of the boarding school was key to a successful and uneventful stay at Munali Secondary School boarding section. Being a novice I arrived as I had been directed to the rooms of the House Captain of May house. It was an experience not easily forgotten. House Captain Mike Chaponda, as I learnt his name was later, questioned me rather demeanly from the steps of his flat. He apparently concluded that I was too small to face the rigor of life in May house. He dismissed me with an instruction to his subordinate to deliver me to David Bailey House. David Bailey house turned out to be less austere. It was a transition hostel for the smaller form 1 students. I found in fact that many of the students there were from the middle class background like me and I found it quite to my liking. David Bailey was located between Young house and Maybin house. Some of the students there were from my Form one class 1F, so I did not feel totally out of place. This was how I was introduced to boarding life at Munali Secondary school and lived it for 5 subsequent years. I made several very close friends during my stay there, some of whom are still close friends to this day. So traumatic was this experience to me that for the first 3 years, I was in boarding I wet my bed every day. Initially I was just afraid to go out and pass urine in the middle of the night. When the light went out at 21:00, thick pitch black darkness descended on the school which would scare the soul out of any home grown 13 year old boy, which I was. So naïve was I, that I thought this would go unnoticed. I soon learnt that there were no secrets in boarding school. I was quickly demoted to sleep on the lower bunker bed, given a bed furthest from the wing monitor and was so stigmatized I lost all my potential friends. My only attraction was that I was still one of the cleverest boys in class. I was also a pretty good chess player. I had started playing chess in grade 6, having learnt it from my elder brother who was then in secondary school. We played frequently at home, and I had become quite proficient. It was a hobby I have kept to this day, my dad always approved, our playing chess, although he did not play himself. He quite astutely understood the superiority of training in logic and reasoning that the game offered.

Boarding life allowed lots of idle time, we spent quite a bit of time playing chess. I lived a lot of life as a boarder as a relative recluse, this was both by nature and worsened off course by my nightly misfortunes. By nature I was an introvert not at all given to the limelight and camaraderie life style demanded by boarding school life style. I recall growing up, that my Aunt on my mum's side coined the Bemba name of "UKu ungutilewa"(shy or timid) which firmly institutionalized my status as a recluse in the family. In form 1, I made friends with Jack Kanyanga and Hector Sikazwe, a pair of very good friends who had a knack for academic competition. Our friendship continued through University and on to adult life. My very best friend though at Munali was an Indian guy called Gurmeet Singh Sohi. His dad was a sports teacher and he had recently been transferred from Chizongwe secondary school to Munali. He was a very candid guy and soon after joining our class came up to me and asked me if I was the cleverest guy in class. We became fast friends.

From form1 to 3, I was in Form 1 F to Form 3F. This was the class that took French as the class option. I found that I did very well in French. In fact one of our French teachers was Mr Sichalwe Kasanda. He subsequently became a lecturer at the University of Zambia in Linguistics, by which time he had a PHD and his title of course changed to Dr Sichalwe Kasanda. He later on became Permanent Secretary in the Ministry of Education. During the period he arranged a programme on the national television, then called ZBS(Zambia Broadcasting Services), called "French For You". Five of my friends and 1, from Form 3 F appeared regularly on that programme which ran for almost one year, once weekly. Talking about French reminds me of a certain Mr Aspinwall. He was an Englishman, who also taught French at Munali. He smoked heavily and was widely suspected of being queer. He was very nice to us and took us to intercontinental hotel, where we watched French movies. Some of which, had dubious content, but were very well attended by the community of French speaking people in Lusaka.

Since I spent a good deal of time at school to which I was quite averse. Holidays were a treat. I lived for holidays. Having moved to Lusaka, not very long back, it took me a while to settle in to the community in woodlands and John Akaplewa road where we lived. We were a family of boys and football was our life from when we were big enough to walk. So we were a big boost to the local boys' football team. We played football, with a money bet on the side between teams, at the football pitch of the neighbourhood church. The Church was called the church of the Nazarene. During one of these games I broke one of the church windows. Feeling too guilty to run, I let myself be hustled home by the local church missionary. When my dad got home I got quite a telling down. It was not a good day.

BOARDING SCHOOL THE NEGATIVE SIDE

Somewhere in the middle term of form 1, a group of guys were transferred into Munali from an unknown boarding school form where, rumour had it they had been expelled. This group promptly gained notoriety at Munali. The group leader was a form 3 student named Mumba Sikumba. Mr Cox Sikumba his father was one of the prominent politicians of the time, a Governor or something.

These guys raided the student dormitories at lights out. All students were forced to open their lockers and hand over any food. The hall prefects conveniently disappeared during these scheduled raids. They would go out of bounds, this meant they left the boarding house without permission and frequently were said to have gone on wild drinking sprees. The whole matter seemed to be too fantastic to believe. In one instances they apparently had gotten into a fight with some University of Zambia students. The University of Zambia being just across the road from Munali, their adversaries had come hunting for them. One of whom it turned out was my elder brother who was studying 2nd year engineering at UNZA at the time. I off course was livid with fear, knowing the reputation of this gang. It turned out though that the reputation of the gang was extremely exaggerated and they were not up to the confrontation. The reputation of the gang declined after that and the school suffered much less from their demeanour.

Well into my form 3, a riot took place at the school. There was disenchantment with the boarding facilities. The Head boy at the time organized the riot.The riot was quickly quelled and the ring leaders expelled. This was followed by a change of the school administration and a disciplinarian headmaster from Chongwe Secondary school called Mr Kulila was brought to the school. There was a relative period of stability and discipline for about 2years subsequently.

My form 3 results were some of the best in the school and I got 8 points.I was selected to Form 4S, which was the pure science class, and the tops students in the school were taken to form 4 S. With increasing academic success I was appointed a sub prefect for the library. Sub prefects were students in form 4, who were selected by the staff in preparation to becoming prefects in form 5. From my early entry into boarding school as a groveling 13year old to a 17year old mature student leader it was an amazing experience. Expecting to become the Library prefect, which was a light hearted job, which kept one entangled in managing the library, suited me very well. However in form 5, the school management decided to create a new position of Vice Captain at David Bailey House, my old transit home. So as fate would have it I was appointed as the Vice Captain for David Bailey. It was a good post with little to do; it allowed me to get to know the frightened young form 1 students very much like I was coming into Boarding School for the first time. Many were like I was naïve and somewhat spoilt. The House Captain was a rather brush guy who took the advantage of his position to defraud the frightened little children of their lavishly packed home food. He was quickly reported and demoted. This is how before I finished form 5 at Munali I became the House Captain of my old House David Bailey, somewhat ironically!!

When the end of year examination came in November 1982 there was a nervous excitement. Those who knew best spoke of great careers and wealth in the years to come. I had not really settled in my mind what to study. My friend Hector Sikazwe and shown interest in studying Architecture at the University of Zambia at Ndola(UNZANDO), as it was then called. It was subsequently called the Copperbelt University. Where, I later became, the first Dean of the School of Medicine, but that's another story. The two week period of the exam proved quite an ordeal. I had embarked on the rather risky strategy of preparing only for 6 of the 9 courses that I was taking. This was risky but gave me enough time to study in the courses in which I really wanted to do well. So when in paper 2 Math exam I inadvertently skipped 4 questions because two papers had been stuck together I was devastated. It was a long nervous wait before I knew my fate the following year in May 1983.

SECONDARY SCHOOL KEY LESSONS

When I entered secondary school in 1978, school was something in my life, by the time I finished in 1982, school was everything. I had learnt that it mattered how well you did in school. It earned you status and respect. I had also learned that to do well in school being smart isn't all it takes. You can be as smart as you like and not do well in school. You most of all, had to have discipline, hard work and strategy. I learnt strategy best of all from Munali Secondary School boarding section. There was a one hour thirty minutes of prep time every day that was compulsory. That was just enough to get any class home work done. Most of my friends did an additional one to two hours between 05:00 and 07:00 in the morning to revise the previous day's class work and generally keep abreast with class work. It was a punishing routine, satisfaction showed on the exam slip result. So from Munali Secondary School I learnt to lose an extra hour of sleep in order to get an extra hour of knowledge. This strategy proved to be a great tactic and I have used it to great advantage now for 32 years!!

The second thing I learnt from school was how to talk. When I got to secondary school I was a shy reclusive boy who only spoke when I was spoken too. While in form 2 at Munali I stumbled upon the Debating Society. It was something completely new to me. It struck a chord and we just clicked together. There was a combination of acting, passion and cold blooded logic that had my name written all over it. Within a few years I became a consummate debater and arguably one of the best debaters in the school. So successful was I that I was chosen the president of the Secondary School Debating Society of Lusaka Province in 1982. So by the time I had finished secondary school I was one of the most accomplished orators you could care to listen too. There were few people who could challenge me to a public debate and win. The third thing I learnt was about leadership. I was always reluctant to lead. It was a position that was thrust upon you at Munali, once you were outstanding in anything, be it sport, smartness or school work. You gravitated to leadership in spite of yourself. The policy appeared to be that the best students were the best leaders. This idea is not without merit. I took advantage of this to mostly to do better in school. Being a prefect allowed you your own room and a little bit more freedom. I found this advantageous for study, so I did not decline the leadership roles which were given to me by the school authorities, though I had little interest in the work itself. I must admit that I was never a good leader myself, but I learnt of this important area, which I pick up later in the story, and I especially observed that some skills were needed to be a good leader. I learnt at least enough to identify a good leader.

So we finished school and waited with baited breath for our fate.

While waiting for the Form 5 results in 1982. My Dad found me a job at the Lusaka City Council in the accounts section. The job involved collecting rates from several points in the city. Our team was located in Lilanda. We were driven from the offices at Civic Center to lilanda every morning and sat in the rather dilapidated offices of the Lilanda Community hall to collect rates from the people living in Lilanda.Lilanda is one of the larger sprawling townships outside Lusaka. It is just after Matero Township on the north side of the city. The population was in excess of 40,000 people.The job was boring, but it paid well. Since I was expecting to go to University the following year it allowed me to save. Sometime during this period an unusual thing happened. My friends and I, while at Munali, had become extremely fond of table tennis. We became pretty good and participated in a number of tournaments. There was a Lusaka Open Table Tennis tournament at Evelyn Hone that year, and being keen to impress my friends with my status as a worker I decided to attend.

Jack Kanyanga was a very clever guy. He still is. I reckon he is one of the cleverest people I know. We had been friends at Munali from David Bailey right to the close of our time there in 1982. He, like me was an avid Table Tennis player and so predictably we met at Evelyn Hone that January in 1983. In those days when mobile phones were unheard off, meeting like that was somewhat unusual in itself. We were all great friends but we were fiercely competitive with each other. So I was very keen to show my friends that, I unlike them, had moved up the social ladder and was working class. Jack like many very clever people was eccentric, his social graces were awkward and like me he was a reticent boy. So when he came up to me looked me straight in the eye and said he had become a "Born Again" Christian, I was quite unsettled. I felt certain something must be wrong. This was a guy who never looked you in the eye unless you challenged him on some obscure theorems of physics like the black hole. His favorite author was Isaac Asimov, an hitherto unknown author, at least by me, a Russian physicist.

My experience of Christianity up to that point was tainted with some cynicism and skepticism. We had a disable female American teacher who was wheel chair bound, at Munali in Form 2. She was a Seventh Day Adventist as well as a "Born Again" Christian. From her I learnt the new words "Seventh Day Adventist" and "Being Born Again". My curiosity was stirred at that time and some spurious conviction lead me to pray what is commonly called the "Sinners Prayer". This I did as frequently as she told us the message of the bible. So I had developed the rather dubious defense against the Christian faith that I had been born again several times. It was something I found amusing and had detracted many who had attempted to direct me to the path over the years. This time the defense fell flat. I felt this idea had been sneaked in and placed in a way that left me defenseless to the message. I was exposed. So impressed was I by Jacks evident transformation, that I decided that whatever it was that had happen to him, I wanted large doses of the same for myself.

This rather obscure event had a significant impact on my life. Before this time I was a predominately uncertain and fearful about the future. My interest in Medicine as a career had been stifled by a rather morbid fear of blood. This experience of the Christian faith turned me around 180 degrees. The experience itself was nothing like I had ever known before. Once all my defenses against this message had dissipated, I began to seek. That day on the 1st January 1983, I experienced Christian conversion. It felt like a heavy weight had been lifted from my shoulders and hoods or scales removed from my eyes. This Christianity thing was real after all. I was totally amazed. My Christian experience has not been easy or smooth, but I have always been convinced that for the first time I came face to face with the message of the bible that day and became a Christian. The Christian author C.S Lewis has written many good books including the Screw Tape Letters and Mere Christianity. He has been one of my favorite writers over the years. The book of his conversion called "Surprised by Grace" is interesting; the last chapter of this book is "Check Mate". On that Saturday afternoon at Evelyn Hone College Hall I had the feeling of having been check mated by God. I always said after that that I had been called by God to be a Doctor, because with my conversion, my aversion to medicine was replaced by a passion for medicine.

UNIVERSITY

In the middle of 1983 the Form 5 results, as it was then called, were published. I nervously went to Munali secondary school notice board to see my results. My heart was pounding when I arrived. There was a small crowd around the notice board. When I found my name I heaved a sigh of relief. My result were among the top five in my school. I had 13 points out of 6 subjects. In those days, that was an excellent result. I got the 2nd best overall result, and my friend Jack got the best points at 11.My elder brother had gotten 16 points, which had been my target to beat.

There was at that time, a new A level school that had been set up in the Copperbelt by the Mining Company ZCCM. Their intention was to train clever young students whom they would sponsor abroad to study in the United Kingdom, and come back to work in the mines. Jack and I were pleased to have been selected for aptitude tests for this premiere class. When we got to Kitwe we were surprised to find almost 200 students had been selected for these tests. They required no more than 50 students. They took us through a rigorous numbers of tests. I met for the first time a guy from Chizongwe Secondary school called Sekelani Banda.We were to become good friends for many years after. Jack and I both passed the aptitude tests and were asked to join the few students who would start the first A level class at Mpelembe Secondary School. It was a tempting offer. My decision turned on one point, the Human Resource Manager a Dr Ng'andu had indicated to my utter surprise, that ZCCM, had enough Doctors, and was unwilling to sponsor anyone wishing to study Medicine. I can't remember Jacks reason; however we both declined the positions offered, and went to study at UNZA instead.

Thus we arrived at University of Zambia Great East Road compass, which was just a walking distance from Munali secondary school. Somewhat conceited with the mistaken belief that we were some of the smartest guys in the country. I quickly learnt that I was wrong on both counts. I entered the School of Natural sciences which is the receiving school for students, wanting to study Medicine, Engineering, and Mining and in those days Agriculture Sciences.I was surprised to find that we were close to 800 students in the first year class of Natural Sciences that year. We were divided into two groups A and B for lectures, as well as tutorial and lab groups. UNZA was an experience.

I stayed at the University in the School of Natural Sciences for 2 years.We had lots of fun, at first probably a little too much. I met up with my old friend Bahavin, and some of the guys I had gone to school with in Kitwe. We took a very casual approach to school, which I quickly learnt was a fatal under estimation of the work out put required. There were parties, Discos and fun times. For some time I forgot my Christian experience, in pursuit of the rewards of working hard in secondary school or so I thought. When my grades in first year began to falter I realized that if I had to make a success of studying Medicine I had to do better.

University was very different from secondary school I found. You were virtually unsupervised by any one. This was a sweet and bitter gift. The fact that you missed lectures at will was fun to start with, but when you had to face the lecturers' questions in exams, it wasn't that much fun. The introduction to university was difficult for me. I found loads of guys much smarter than me and a lot harder working. There were guys like Elijah Chaila, with whom I later became very good friends. Kelly Chibale, who got a distinction in Chemistry, and later went to Oxford, or Cambridge University, he subsequently became a very distinguished Professor at the University of Cape town in South Africa. During the course of the first year I mellowed and began the odious task of catching up for the loads of work missed in term 1. It was an experience I would not be keen to repeat. When the end of year exam came I got 2B+s and 2Bs.We were studying 4 courses M110 Mathematics,BZ110 Biology,C110 Chemistry and P110 Physics.These were introductory courses similar to the first year of A levels taught in some high schools abroad. Nowadays off course by many private schools as well. The competition to get into the Medical Quota as it was called was stiff. Only 45 places were available. Luckily I was selected and was extremely relieved. Many of my friends, who had worked much harder than I, had not been selected. Many were disillusioned and left University altogether.

Lessons from first year

First year of University was a year of discovery to me and I let myself go. There was much that was appealing about life at the University. For a young 18 year old boy it was all that dreams are made off. We got pocket money from the Government Bursaries, which though not generous was more than I had ever had before, except for my brief working experience. By the end of first year all my good secondary school principles had dissipated and my social life was such that my school life had been eroded. My friend Jack, who had remained true to his Christian faith, was a great help in getting me back to Christian ways. I, up to then, had mistakenly believed that the biggest hurdle to a good time was secondary school. I quickly learnt that I had sorely been mistaken. The next thing I learnt was that there where many young people like me, many much more intelligent than I, so the mere fact that I had managed to enter University impressed no one at the University. Though it appeared a big achievement to me to the rest it was only the invitation card to the party, or being lined on the marks for a race. It was a race for sure, you had to jostle, hustle and work to get to the finish line. I also learnt that much more discipline was required to do well, more hard work and more brains than secondary school needed. You see, I quickly realized that at secondary school, we were leaning on the teachers for our learning. In University the teaching is not personalized, its mob teaching, there was no one to lean on but you.

THE UNZASU STRIKE

The Vice Chancellor in 1983 at UNZA was Dr Jacob Mwanza, who later became Governor of the Bank of Zambia. The University had a federal system, with two campuses at Lusaka and Ndola with Principals'. The UNZANDO, principals was Prof Mubanga Kashoki, who later became a good friend of mine, and Professor Kashwaka Mwauluka was principal at UNZA Main Campus. Prof Kashoki was a linguistic, who specialized in Bemba. Prof Mwauluka was a biologist. The students rather mischievously called him "the frog dissector". Prof Mwauluka was decidedly unpopular among the students. His care of the University surrounding was meticulous, and the greens shown with exuberance. He was perceived as rather distanced from the students and the staff. In our secondary school days at Munali, the exploits of the students at UNZA were legendary. In 1983, I found myself in the centre of one of those legendary student riots.The student movement in those days was extremely militant. Even then, the number of students at UNZA main campus was 10,000 strong, which is about 50% of what it is now.

My brother who was more experienced than I, in these matters was in his final year in the school of Engineering. We were both living in Kwacha house, in the old residences, commonly called the ruins. The whirlwind of events leading to the actual strike fail me precisely, however the student body was always restless towards exam time. It was nearing the end of year exams, there was a sense of desperation in the air as "Mwauluka's Axe was looming". This the common lingua franca of the time, which meant exams were nearby and those who failed were literal considered to have been cut off by the head of the institution. So any students' distresses were accentuated. The trigger may have been the meals which were deteriorating in quality or the government bursary which was somewhat low and often given late. The politics of the days was always dragged in to give a national appeal to the grievance. Whichever the case some brewing unrest fermented and the UNZASU president took the podium to bravely indicate they would be no more classes until these problems were resolved. My brother advised me to pack my bags. Which I dutifully did, with some bemusement and disbelief. For the first two days running battles were fought from students' hostels to the university campus streets with riot police keeping vigil on the campus. Either party caught in the territory of the other was duly punished. Molotov cocktails (petrol bombs) were thrown from the hostels to the streets and tear gas canister came back into the hostels as a prompt response.

Two days later we found ourselves besieged by paramilitary officers. These guys looked like they had come in for a full fledged war. They segregated the campus into 3 zones, sealing off students in their rooms. There were over 200 paramilitary officers in full riot gear. In those days' authoritarianisms was enforcement with brutal force with no reluctance at all. My watch was telling me it was 05:00, in the morning when the unit commander was announcing in very disheveled English that we had 10 minutes to exit our rooms, before we were forcibly evicted. By the time the morning news was announcing that the University had been closed. We were doing frog jumps from Kwacha house to the Goma lakes in front of the campus with our luggage in tow. Before 10:00 in the morning buses were dispatching students to various destinations in the city. That year the University stayed closed for almost 3 months. Several student were suspended and expelled. I learnt that quite a number had been injured and a few interred (jailed).

Second Year

Second year was somewhat of a blur. I had been exhausted by the work required to get into the Medical Quota as it was called. When we got into the second year, many of us were more than a little disappointed. The second year was a lot more tedious than the first year, it consisted of an additional year in the School of Natural Sciences doing intermediate courses in Biology and Chemistry. There was BZ210,BZ220, C220 and C240. I found these courses were laborious and boring in the extreme. The chemistry courses were a little more bearable I found. The biology course and their practical's were truly unbearable. Sometime in the first term, I took the somewhat courageous decision to stop attending lectures and labs in BZ210, which was animal biology or entomology (the study of insects) or perhaps both. This was certainly a foolish decision and almost proved my undoing. I spent a good deal of my time in my room simply copying notes from my friends who attended the lecturers. Which, I did not bother to read. It was a decision which I would not encourage anyone to take. It was both naïve and reckless. Not knowing this I was smug in myself confidences and encouraged many of my friends to do the same. The staff of the school and the course probably didn't notice or most likely couldn't care less. My labs which were all copied from my friends who attended the labs got flying grades. So we were all none the wiser.

However two weeks before the end of year exam, I discovered my folly, when I began to study for the exams. I had books of perfectly copied notes which I had meticulously filed under the various biology courses. When I tried reading through the notes none of it made a whole lot of sense. It was the classification of species, animals, and plants. The notes were poorly taken, in very bad English; the scientific names were poorly spelt. It dawned on me that I had very badly miscalculated. No one was willing or interested in my plight which was self induced. Everyone was busy doing revision and none of my friends were willing to lend me or probably had any better notes. I was in despair. To get into Medical School the following year I was required to maintain a minimum of B grades in all the biology and Chemistry courses. My position was that I could hardly pass using the notes I had, let alone get B grades. So stressed was I over this that I began to neglect all the rest of the courses and was at risk of failing all the courses. Being a Christian in good standing, I got together some of our senior Christians in the University Christian fellowship for some help. One of the mature ladies in the group offered some counseling support and prayer. When exams time came, I was still very nervous and anxious. The examination proved very difficult. It turned out that the materials were difficult for everyone. When the exam results were posted I got 2 Bs and 2 B+ s in second year I was overwhelmed. It turned out that the BZ210 paper had been so difficult all the results had been up graded. Whatever the case I breathed a sigh of relief and promised never to make such a mistake in my studies again, and I never did!! I learnt my lesson and I learnt it well.

UNZA MEDICAL SCHOOL

When I arrived at Medical School at Ridgeway campus which was just across the road from the University Teaching Hospital I was prepared to work very hard. My experience in my first 2 years had been unpleasant. So I determined to work hard at Medical School. The Medical School Training ran for a period of 5 years. In addition to 2 years of natural Sciences this was a total of 7 years. In 1985 when I started Medical Training, the course had 2 years of Basic Science training and 3 years of clinical science training. In those days it was like being thrown into a turbulent running stream with cold water and just trying to survive. Medical Training in any environment is hard enough; the structure of the programme at UNZA SOM did not make it any easier. The materials were both voluminous and complex at the same time. The emphasis I learnt latter when I got enough time to think about it, was to learn about normal Human body structures in year 1 of the medical course and then abnormalities of body structures and their assessment in year 2. I was oblivious to this fact and was preoccupied with learning the material and surviving medical school. Since I had already decided to become a Surgeon, I throw my energies into studying Anatomy. Anatomy is the science of body structures. I was latter to become a lecturer in Anatomy, but that's' something I'll say more about latter. My intention was to be the best Surgeon I could be. By the end of my first year in Medical school I was among the top five students in class overall, and one of the best students in Anatomy.

The Medical School was very different from the Main Campus as we called the Main University Campus which was located in Kalundu area about 5kilometre from the Medical school on Great East Road Lusaka. The Ridgeway Campus was initially part of the School of Education and was used for distance education.It was located at the corner of Nationalist road and government road in Ridgeway area. When the Medical School was opened in 1966, it was considered ideal for the Medical School, because it was just opposite the University Teaching

Hospital, which is a 2,500 bed hospital. This meant that the main University Campus and the Medical school campus where in separate locations (this is the case to the present day), by virtue of the necessity to train medical students using the hospital as a key component of the practical training.

Several things struck me as unusual about the place. Every morning at 06:00, we would wake to the noise of mourners. Visiting hours for patients was from 06:00 to 07:00 in the morning. The School is directly opposite the childrens hospital, the pediatric section. We were initially in B block which was on the furthest side of the campus away from the hospital. However we could still hear daily the crying of the bereaved for their lost children. The daily crying was a wakeup call for me, to do my best to become a doctor as soon as I could. So I could be there to help that crying mother, by saving her baby it was clarion call for me, to work and learn the art well.

We lived in shared rooms, with four students to a room. Our 3rd year class was considered small with 39 students. The lecture rooms were within the residences and were actually more like tutorial rooms. The second striking thing was my experience of the dissecting room. Anatomy is one of the sciences essential to medicine. Traditionally the practical component of the course consists of time spent dissecting preserved human bodies called cadavers. We had heard about this practice before we got to medical school. Many of us were anxious about it and slightly nervous. There were many theories about the reason for this among our lay non medical students friends. One of which was that this was a way to remove the fear of death from the medical trainee and make it possible to treat disease in an impassionate way. Some said it was a rite of passage. If you fainted you would automatically be sent back to the School of Natural Sciences as lacking the caliber to do the medical course. With all this background chatter and gossip I was keen to still my emotions sufficiently to pass the test of the dissecting room experience, if indeed it was a test.

When the Professor of Anatomy who was called Chatruvedi ushered us into the Anatomy Dissecting room, there was stillness in the room. The room itself was intimidating enough. There were Air Conditioners against all four walls that gave a deadly chill to the place. The body's were clad in black polythene bags and mounted on dissecting tables spread across the dissection hall. We hurdled around the door nervously ready to make a quick exit. He divided us into 8 to 10 groups and had us stand around our designated cadaver (which is the technical name for the preserved body used for medical dissection).None was laughing. He had us uncover the bodies. It was an ordeal not easily forgotten. It took 3 days for the class to recover from the experience. Many of us refused to eat meat for a few days after that. I was proud that if this was the test for the mental attitude required to do the Medical course I had at least passed. I remember thinking, the day of reckoning had come, and did I really have what it takes to be a doctor. My spirit quivered a little, I grit my teeth and knew I had come too far to back out now. Whatever it took, I had to do it. The crying of the mother for their lost babies in the Childrens ward echoed in my mind and reassured me. I was resolute in my conviction even though for the first time I was afraid.

It dawned on me then the seriousness of what it meant to study medicine. If it was necessary in training Doctors to desecrate the dead, in this way, then the Doctors work was truly onerous. In that moment I learnt, the first rule of Medicine, to practice Medicine well you must let the body yield all its secrets to you, only then can you resolve its ailments well.

Within one month the somber experience of the dissecting room had faded, and the banter, ill behavior and general indifference had set in. Many of us were eating sweets and all types of food stuff in the DR as it was called. Life in medical school was challenging but lots of fun. I mixed with lots of intelligent people among the staff and students, some of whom I'll describe in the course of the story.

The Medical course ran for 5 years at the Ridgeway campus. In the first two years we were confined to the campus itself and the labs within the campus. In the subsequent 3 years we took our lectures in the hospital, and spent most of our time shadowing doctors within the hospital. The first 2 years were somewhat boring, and I got the feeling somebody was giving me the run around. I felt like the subject of a practical joke, where somebody makes you think that you are studying medicine only to discover that it was all a joke and you were in fact on a course studying some obscure human science of no real consequence. I think many of my friends felt the same frustration.

Fortunately the course materials were so heavy it gave us very little time to reflect. There was also the constant fear of failure. No one dared to let their guard down, lest that be the means by which their demise might come. When we have finished the first year we had worked through physiology- the study of body functions, Anatomy the study of body structures, Biochemistry the study of how individual cells use chemical substances and pathways to achieve these body function s and to spice it up human psychology- or understanding how people think and behave.

I shared my room in 3rd year with 2 other guys. One of whom struggled immensely with the course and eventually had to repeat, while the other guy was a conscientious and studious fellow. He was a lanky guy and somewhat of a ladies' man. Lamios Munthali told lots of interesting stories of his days as a young boy in Ndola rural. It was intriguing and sometimes unbelievable to imagine him walking to school in Ndola rural and struggling to learn math on the school floor. He achieved amazing success and became a consultant pathologist in the United Kingdom. We got on very well. I spent a good deal of my time in those days among the Christian group at the campus. The group was called Ridgeway Christian fellowship. It was a small group compared to the total population of the campus, somewhere close to 35 to 40 students. I learnt a lot about Christianity, Christians and the Christian faith.

Some of our lecturers at the time were people of exceptional ability. Our physiology lecturer in particular was a great teacher. He had a booming loud voice with a heavy Tonga accent. His dressing was not untypical of his upbringing. He made the physiology come alive and he had a way of forcing you to think on your feet. Dr Chijikwa. Biochemistry was taught by Dr Gondwe and Dr Mary Zulu. Dr Mary Zulu became the Registrar of the Health Professions Council of Zambia. Our Professor of Anatomy was a legend. He came to the school towards the end of our course. Our Anatomy programme had been extremely bad. The professor who had been in charge of the course had just retired. The Dean of the school Professor Mukelebai (He was Dr Mukelebai at the time) was hard pressed to find a replacement. With the result, that we were lumbered with an ill tempered clinician who had a rather coarse knowledge of Anatomy. He came in briefly each morning , shouted some basic instructions and did a demonstrative dissection, in which we had no idea what he was doing and left. This was our rather erratic introduction to Gross Anatomy. We had no lectures in Histology- the study of body structures under the microscope, or of embryology- the study of the development of body structures. The experience taught me that teaching is an art. There are those who have the knack for it and those who don't. Our clinician clearly did not have the knack for it but, boy Professor Joseph Karashani had a knack for teaching Anatomy. When Professor Karashani came in our third term, we were well on our way to knowing very little organized Anatomy. He was an excellent teacher and completely well rounded in the teaching of anatomy. Within one term we recovered sufficiently to complete Anatomy in our first year with a respectable level of knowledge in all the branches of Anatomy. Professor Karashani had a prolific memory. He not only knew everybody by name, which are surname, middle name and first name. But quite exceptionally also could remember all the computer numbers and all the handwritings of all the students. He was also an excellent organist and became the chief organist for the main Anglican Church at the centre of the city. He was truly inspirational to an impressionable young man like myself at the time. I decided then to study Anatomy, as a means to being a good surgeon. It was decision which I have never regretted, then or since.

By the time I was finishing my 3rd year at the school of Medicine I was extremely shy and felt awkward around women. I had spent 5 years in an all boy's school at Munali, which certainly did not help. With the increasing amount of work at the Medical school I found no time to correct that vulnerability. I had reached about 20year of age and I felt increasingly paralyzed by this deficiency which everybody appeared to notice. I could sense that people were constantly giving me awkward looks, which suggested that I wasn't quite with it. I was eventually categorized as overly studious, religious recluse with a stilted social life.

In our 3rd year psychology was taught as two half course (PS251 and PS252), these courses were taught by the department of psychology at the Great East Road campus. The Head of Psychology was Dr Peter Machungwa who later in 1991 became a cabinet minister in the MMD government. I barely failed my psychology (PS252) and was asked to see him over this in 1985. He was an affable man who reassured me that since this was a half course and the fail was marginal I could continue my training.

When we got into 4th year we moved from the Normal body sciences (Anatomy,Physiology,Biochemistry and Psychology) to the abnormal ones(Pathology,Microbiology and Pharmacology). We also moved from A block which had shared rooms to B block which had single rooms. The 4th year courses were a lot more voluminous and required more brawn than brain. Our pathology lecturer was Dr Patil who was also the hospital pathologist. We had several lecturers in Microbiology and we were required to do a number of practical's. One of our Pharmacology lecturers was a beautiful lady called Miss Lewanika. She was almost always late for her lectures. The guys in the class enjoyed her lectures, less because of its content, but more because of the lecturer herself. The girls were less pleased. We attended 1or 2 postmortems during our pathology course. Having done 1 year of gross Anatomy dissections, the post mortems where a less intimidating affair than we had expected. In my 4th year it was becoming increasingly difficult to go to church at Northmead Assemblies of God in Northmead. It was a walk of 30minutes across town from Ridgeway to Northmead and back. Having also became more acquainted with Christian friends from the Baptist Church who were at the medical school, I eventually decided to start attending the Baptist church at

Kabwata. It was a newly established church which was congregating at the community hall near Kabwata Market. Elijah Chaila was one of my class mates, was a regular at Lusaka Baptist Church on Lubu road Longacres.He later became a Consultant Neurologist in Ireland. Over the 5 years I was at the medical school I was quite regular at Kabwata Baptist church, eventually becoming a member in about 1988. We had a small Christian group at the Medical School called the Ridgeway Christian fellowship. Some of the regulars in those days were Roland Msiska, Clement Chela,Simon Mphuka and Henry Mugala.Many of whom subsequently became renowned doctors in different medical specialties in Zambia and abroad.

I always felt unduly restrained by the course from getting a real fill of medicine. One felt that all the study course was doing was discouraging any would be applicants from studying Medicine. Our colleagues who were in the clinical years of study assured us that we would soon come out of purgatory and would enter the bliss of clinical science training. I think we were all feeling the exhaustion of the experience by fourth year. I graduated in 1988 as one of the top students in my class with a credit in the Bachelor of Science Human biology course. There were five other guys in my class who got credits, these were Elijah Chaila who won the best student award, Ashraf Coovadia, Roy Chuunga,Sekelani Banda,Joe Yikona and Ajoy Chaabra. Ashraf Coovadia became Consultant Pediatrician at the University of Wistwaterand in South Africa, Roy migrated to south Africa, Sekelani Banda became like me a clinical Anatomist and eventually Dean /Deputy Vice Chancellor of Cavendish Medical School, Joe Yikona migrated to the United Kingdom doing Internal Medicine and Geriatrics in Cambridge and Ajoy Chaabra to Texas in the USA.

In 1988 we crossed the Nationalist road and went into our clinical training part of the course. It was a relief that I had finally began real medical training after almost 16 years in school it was an exhausting experience. I also changed my digs and moved into C block, which was the building adjoining A block . A block was furthest from the hospital and D block, which was next to C Block, was nearest the childrens block entrance to the hospital. We also now wore Doctors coats and had shinning new Littman's stethoscopes which we hang proudly round our necks. It was fun on the hospital wards to be mistakenly called Doctor by unsuspecting patients and staff.

The clinical training was done at the University teaching hospital which was a 2,500 bed hospital across the road from the school of medicine campus. It consisted of a 3 year attachment to one of the four major departments in turn (Medicine, Surgery, Obstetrics and Gynaecology and Pediatrics) for 2 years. There was a junior year in 5th year which was introductory and a senior year in 7th year which was an advanced training. In the sandwich year of 6th year rotations in Medical and surgical subspecialties were done. This consisted of rotations in the larger subspecialties of surgery such as Ophthalmology(Eye Surgery), Ear Nose and Throat(Surgery of the internal organs of the face), Orthopaedics(Surgery of Bones),Facial Maxillary Surgery (Surgery of the Bone structures of the face and Jaw) and Anaesthesia (The branch of Medicine that deals with putting patients to sleep for operations).Similarly Medicine specialties included rotations in Radiology(The branch of medicine which deals with preparing and reading X rays),Dermatology(Skin Diseases) and STIs (Sexual transmitted Diseases) as well as Forensic Medicine(The branch of medicine that deals with investigating causes of death especially due to crime). The rest of the year was spent in Psychiatry (Diseases of the mind or madness) and Public Health(Prevention of disease).

The clinical rotations were arranged in 8 week cycles with the 9th week being an examination week. We were broken into 4 groups by the 4 main departments. Each group was broken into 4 to 5 units (hospital teams of Doctors working under the supervision of a senior Doctor called a consultant) following the number of clinical units in each department. The training consisted largely of a practical clinical training in which we were integrated into the clinical units from about 09:00 to 11:00 in the morning. From 08:00 to 09:00 we had lectures from each department in turn. From 11:00 to 12:00 there were departmental tutorials (interactive small group teaching). In the afternoon we had seminars and presentations organized by departments.

During the course of my training we moved from John Akapelwa road in Woodlands to Zambezi way in Jesmondine. I spent a good deal of time at the Medical School and was hardly ever at home except for short 1 to 2 week holidays. In about 1988, my Dad was transferred from the Lusaka City council to Mwense Rural council. He was preparing for his retirement. My financial situation was also declining at the time. My elder brother had finished his Engineering Course and having initially worked for the Mines in Chililabombwe had transferred back to Lusaka. He was able to provide me some monthly support which was a great help in tidying me over the rough patches left by a rather low government bursary. Some of the family moved to Mwense and about half of the children stayed to finish school or for work. The family fragmented and the times became harder. I in turn was feeling the pressure of studying for so long without any clear income in site. Having come all this way I decided to work harder so that I could finish my course and start paying my own way. The pay for Doctors at the time was the equivalent of about 300USD per month. Many of our colleagues were already talking of migrating at the time.

My first attachment to the University Teaching Hospital in Lusaka was in Obstetrics and Gynaecology. What someone has called "Diseases of Women and Pregnancy". In the first 2 years of medical training we had some familiarity, with the hospital, but only from a distant. It was like meeting a cousin for the first time, whom you had heard a lot about. It was exciting, intriguing and mysterious all in one. Most of all I felt that at last I had arrived into the real training for becoming a doctor. If I had a choice in the training of Doctors I would advise that the first year of practical training should be in Internal Medicine (General Disease of Adults). This I say from experience. When a team of 10 naïve medical students walked onto the Obstetric and Gynaecological wards in B block at the UTH, it felt like we had been thrown onto a train that was running at 100 kilometres an hour with people getting on and off in rapid succession. You also felt stark naked, with all sorts of people giving you quizzical looks as they proceeded about their business.

I learnt latter that the department had some structure and organization to it. I did not think so at the time. We were very coarsely divided among the 4 firms in the department and told to go find the consultant in charge. My first question was what is a firm? and my second equally naïve, what is a consultant? Fortunately I kept the questions to myself. Someone who looked like they had worked in the place for sometime advised us to see the head of department. After many false leads we finally run into the Head of the department of Obstetrics and Gynaecology.He was doing his rounds. This I learnt latter meant he was seeing his patients on the hospital wards. We found him on the B21 ward. He was gruff and rather disheveled. Not at all like what I had expected. He appeared ill tempered and was quite indifferent to us. He repeated the same instructions we had been given earlier. However he added one thing, for good measure, which was new. "I don't like being followed by students". He was surrounded by what looked to me like a hoard of adoring youngish Doctors. This team I learnt was the equivalent of what was called a firm. That is a group of doctors working under one senior doctor who worked as a team providing a unified clinical service to the department. It amounts to a squadron in a military Air force or a company in Army terms. The only difference was that unlike the military where the head was a junior officer in the medical system the head is equivalent to a four star General.The term for this tyrannical figure was "Consultant". The consultant was genu flexed to and treated with equal reverence to a four star General. We cowered under this assault and scampered pretending to do what we had been told. So was our introduction to clinical medicine.

The department was arranged into two subsections, Obstetric section and the Gynaecology section. The Obstetric section dealt with pregnant women and delivery, while the gynaecological section dealt with disease of the female system and problems in early pregnancies less than 3 months. The labour ward was the most interesting area. This was where women gave birth. In those days before the clinics in Lusaka had developed facilities for delivery, most deliveries were done at UTH. There were close to 50 deliveries a day. Each student was expected to perform 10 deliveries over the 9 week attachment. The labour ward was L shaped and arranged in order of progression of labour. Labour, I learnt in medical terms did not mean work as is the common understanding. For example the Ministry of Labour, which deals with employment. It meant the process of delivering a baby that starts when the uterus (the womb) begins to have muscle contractions. The first room was where the initial assessment of pregnant women was done by the midwife. The midwife is a nurse trained in assisting women in child birth. The pregnant woman is sent to the next room if she is in the early stage of labour. In the late or final stage of labour the adjoining suite which had special labour beds were used. The room that followed was called the special observation unit. This was where women with pregnancies which were likely to be difficult were kept. All these rooms were on the left side of the corridor from the admission room. On the right was where post partum women (those who had already delivered) were kept in. Next to this were cribs for the new borns.

I quickly learnt the art of delivering a normal pregnancy. It required some skill courage and a thick apron. On a number of occasions when labour progressed quickly I was splash with liquor, the fluid that surrounds the baby in the womb. The head of our firm was Mr David Chikamata. He was called "Mister" and not "Doctor", I learnt latter, because he studied in the United Kingdom for his specialist training in Obs and Gyn. The UK system historically started with the procedures requiring operations being referred to a group of barbers. Barbers were as they are now, people who were skilled with knives. Over the years the group of barbers also became trained as Doctors and created their associations of barbers. They retained the initial historical title of Mister. Therefore in the surgical specialties in the UK, the title Mister signified that you were not only a Doctor but had done specialist training and were listed as a member of the College of Surgeons, which was what the Association of Barbers was eventually called. Many commonwealth countries copied the system and those countries that had Doctors trained in the United Kingdom returned to their home countries using these peculiarly British titles. You can well imagine that being one of the few Fellows of the Royal College of Obs and Gyn (FRCOG), Mr Chikamata was well respected. He was an impressive Consultant, his dress was immaculate and his knowledge in the field consummate. Following each call day, when our unit which was Firm B, was on call there was a hand over round. This I learnt was when one consultant tells the other consultant what had been done the previous night and what was left over, in terms of the labour ward work. The team of two units breezed through the labour ward in what could only be called an academic foray. Even though I was green behind the ears and my knowledge of the field was very raw, I found it a great pleasure. Mr Chikamata conducted the event with panache and finesse which I have rarely seen then and since. I was caught out myself several times by his very incisive reasoning in clinical obstetrics. The key was a clear understanding of what was then called Philpot's' partogram. This was described by Hugh Philpot's in 1972, who worked in Zimbabwe. He was a good Christian gentleman, and we had the privilege of meeting Prof Philpot at our Christian fellowship meeting in the 1980s. The partogram is a graphic representation of the progress of labour. This is measured by two key features, which are the descent of the baby in the womb and the extent of opening of the cervix, or the neck of the womb. The rate of progress of these two features determine the need for medical intervention, in the progress of labour in any women admitted in the labour ward. The round constituted a total of between 15 to 20 people. This included undergraduate medical students, postgraduates and all the clinical staff. We learnt a very high level of obstetrics and gynaecology in those high tension rounds conducted by Mr Chikamata. In the final week of the course we had clinical exams. The external examiner was from the Mine Hospital and his name was Mr Godfrey Katema. He later became the director of the University Teaching hospital. The exams consisted of 3 short cases and one long case. This meant that the examiners presented patients on the ward with either gynaecological or obstetric conditions on which you were asked to make a spot diagnosis or perform a specific task under their direct observation. Subsequently this form of examination became less common because it was said, of its lack of objectivity. My long case was a patient with a VVF (Vesical Vaginal Fistula). This condition is common in Africa and results in abnormal communication between the bladder and the vagina. This often is the result of a baby stuck in the birth passage for too long. I was nervous. My examiners were Mr Sikazwe, who was a consultant and Mr Katema who was external examiner. They asked me to do a speculum examination. This is an instrument that is used to visualize the vaginal wall as well as the cervix (the neck of the womb). The patient took one look at me and one look at the Sims speculum and became very anxious. My hands were unsteady and I dropped the speculum. The examiners were gracious and lead me in a discussion on the signs and symptoms of VVF. When the day was done I was exhausted and very sure I had failed the exam. Happily when the results came I managed a bare pass. I was elated.

My next junior clinical rotation was in Internal medicine or Adult medicine. The wards are located in E block which has 3 floors. The Building is shaped like a V, with the male wards on your left as you entered the landing and the female wards on your right. The male wards are prefixed with the number 1 while the female wards with the number 2. I'm pretty sure this must have been done in the days before gender became a topical issue. The first number indicates the floor and the second the type of patient, that is male or female.So E01 was the male Medical ward on the ground floor, E12 on the other hand was the female ward on the first floor. Each ward had four cubicles with, 2 sideward and what was called a dayroom. Each cubicle had 6 beds, except for the last cubicle which was longer and had in total of about 12 beds. On average a medical ward had about 50 to 60 patients. In total the medical ward had close to 300 beds. At the time in 1988, the HIV epidemic was just beginning to have its effect.The first cases having just been reported in Zambia in about 1986. The medical wards were beginning to get the main impact of the increasing incidences of TB and its complications. The medical rotations was poorly organized. If the obstetric department had been confusing the medical ward was worse.There was no organized system of teaching in the department.The head of department was Dr Wadawhan, a lean Asian man, who had a bitter expressionless look in his eye.I wandered if he suffered from peptic ulcer disease. We learnt very little in the rotation. In the senior years with the help of the British government a number of British Physicians joined the department and this went some way in improving the departmental teaching. Two Doctors were legendary in failing students at the time. One was Dr Bissearu, who was an Indian

Doctor trained in England. He was MRCP. This meant he was a Member of the Royal College of Physicans. He had so many other additional qualifications we were sure he knew everything there was to know in internal Medicine. Unfortunately for us I thing his best teaching days were behind him. He was rather forgetful. Ill-tempered and had a tendency of being verbose. What little medicine we learnt was from the energetic young postgraduate students of the time. One of the star students of the time was Dr David Namushi, he eventually migrated to Ireland and became a consultant in respiratory medicine. The end of term examinations were terrible, because having learnt so little, I had very little to show the examiner. The format was similar to the Obs and Gyn rotation with one long case and a couple of short cases. We had two sets of examiners in each type of case. I donot know how I did it but I was happy to just pass the examination in the last week of the rotation.

We started the surgery clerkship as these attachments were called in the 3 rd quarter of 1988. The countries economy was in decline, and the government of UNIP which had been in power for two decades was faced with an increasing burden of disease with a declining health budget. There had been a number of strikes by junior doctors over low pay. Many had been frustrated and left the country. There were many of my friends who felt they had been ill advised to choose a career in medicine. Many had intentions of migrating as soon as they completed the training. In this rather dejected environment I started my surgical attachments.

Having always wanted to be a cardiothoracic surgery, I was very excited about the surgical rotation. I recall that I was attached to yellow firm. Yellow firm was run by the head of the department of surgery Professor Ann Bailey. She was a British trained surgeon and It was said that she was an Anglican nun. Though I myself saw no evidence of this. She was a tyrannical figure and ran rough shod over the staff and students. In years that followed she gained international renown as one of the early researchers in the then little known HIV related Kasposi Sarcoma. This is a malignant cancer of the vascular system which had previously been described by a Hungarian surgeon (Moritz

Kaposi), but was an indolent disease before the advent of HIV infection.

I recall that her rounds started with a stroll from the entrance of G21 to the last cubicle. She had a shrill voice and if anything was out of place and patients not exposed for the round the sister in charge would have it. So everyone, was nervous before her teaching rounds. Most of all, the medical students, who were all green behind the ears. The department though, proved much better organized than medicine. There appeared in fact to be many more staff and many subsections or specialties under surgery. We had departmental tutorials and took part in staff departmental meetings. There were many Zambian surgeons of renown. Mr Lupando Munkonge was head of Red Firm; the units in surgical departments were called firms. I'm not sure why. Mr Munkonge eventually became head of department and later Dean of the school of Medicine. He was an amusing lecturer, he punctuated his lectures with several "Bemba" phrases. He was grandfatherly and a very lenient examiner. The Senior Registrar, who I learnt was next in rank to the consultant, in yellow firm, was Mr Ezingansian Krikor. Mr Krikor it was rumored, was a retired military Doctor from one of the East block countries. He was an excellent surgeon, but very coldly aloof and somewhat of a recluse. He too eventually became head of Surgery after Mr Munkonge and subsequently became Professor of Surgery. Most of the surgeons of the time were trained in the United Kingdom and were fellows of the College of Surgeons of Edinburgh. There are 3 surgical Colleges in the UK, the RCS England, Edinburgh and Glasgow. Whereas, the College of Physicians was only one. The RCS England is generally regarded as the most prestigious I later learnt. I came into contact with a young upcoming surgeon who was just completing his training at the time called Yakub Mulla. Dr Mulla, who was to influence my career in surgery tremendously,. He was among the second stream of graduates in the newly introduced Master of Medicine programme at the University. The university had decided to start its own local specialist training in Zambia, to reduce the high costs of training doctors abroad and the low returns. We were all as medical students very unhappy with this both because we thought the training was of a low quality, but also because we felt it would make it difficult to go abroad. In fact the government announced that no scholarships would be provided to study for any programmes for which local training programmes existed. This, I now think, was a very prudent decision, although I like everyone else did not think so at the time. We all agreed at the time that this was the worst statement to come out of cabinet office. We, many of us, at the time, had the secret intentions to migrate abroad. The economics at the time were so bad and conditions of services so low, that many of the consultants used the local minibus that run in front of the hospital to get to and from work. This would be considered extremely abnormal now, but was the order of the day. Sometime in the 1990s the Ministry of Health was forced to buy government vehicles for all Zambian consultants to redress this. This occurred about the time Mr Michael Sata became Minister of Health.

Dr Mulla had a reputation of being an extremely good student with excellent surgical skills. Being good medical students, we were well up on all the gossip of the day, who was what and who trained where, and who was a good doctor. Dr Mulla was seen as tops, so we were all keen to attend his tutorials. Along with him there were at least 4 postgraduate students I recall being in the department at the time. These were Dr Muyendekwa, Dr Chadwick Ngwisha, Dr Duncan Mugala and Dr Mohammed Essa. Dr Mulla subsequently went to the UK to study orthopeadics eventually becoming Professor of Orthopaedics and Trauma. He also, as I recount later, became Dean of the School of Medicine.

I hated urology in particular. The Urologists at the time was a Mr Elem. He was Asian but a naturalized British citizen. He was an excellent urologist, with an excellent research profile. He was also rather egotistical and somewhat ungracious to the Zambian psyche. He made it clear that he felt the Zambian behavior too circuitous, slow and lacking in a sense of urgency. We had bed side tutorials once a week which were totally unnerving. His questions were direct and punishing. Failure to answer preciously resulted in a humiliating dressing down. Many of the young female students were brought to tears by this academic onslaught. His senior Registrar was Dr Francis Manda who had recently returned from specialist training in East Germany. He was a handsome man and drove a fancy sports car which was the envy of all the students. It fuelled every body's belief, that the best thing to do after graduation, was to go and work in Europe. I found the surgery rotation extremely interesting in addition to the ward work there was a twice weekly foray into the surgical operating room. I never got over the excitement of watching a surgical operation. I felt that at last I had arrived. My only disappointment was with the lack of depth in the surgical teaching. Even as a junior medical student I sensed that surgical teaching lacked the vigor and depth that I had expected. The surgical practice struck me as overly simplistic and lacking in scientific depth.I learnt that this varied from firm to firm.We learnt that some of our friends in blue firm were having great teaching. So many of us, sneaked in to their ward rounds with Mr Chris Bem. He was a British surgeon, who with his wife had recently qualified as fellows of the RCS, his wife from the Faculty of Anesthesia of the RCS. He was brimming with surgical knowledge but less so when it came to surgical skills. My first surgical exam was a big disappointment; I barely managed a C+.

I remember the first lecture Mr Chris Bem gave to our fifth year class.It was on burns. I had long made up my mind then to become a surgeon, with the FRCS title after my name. So when we were informed that Mr Chris Bem would give us the lecture on burns, I was very expectant. It turned out to be rather less than I expected. It must have been his maiden lecture, because he was clearly very nervous. The content was fair, but perhaps he had not quite expected such a large audience. He got better over the years and proved a very hard working surgeon.

My final rotation was in pediatrics and child health. The pediatric wing was located a little away from the main hospital, but within the same building. It had a gate directly opposite the student residences, and was therefore very accessible from the rooms. By the time I started the 9 week attachment my enthusiasms for clinical work was less than what it had been earlier. I had discovered to my loss that there is romance in medicine as there is in courtship, but that phase passes. Once you get down to it there is some brutal hard work that is required and I had began to experience this. I had no special liking for pediatrics. The rotation itself was particularly poorly organized. Unlike surgery the students were somewhat of an after thought and relegated to ward errands by the unit Doctors. This was probably because of the critical shortage of doctors and the heavy burden of newborn, infant and childhood disease. The infant mortality and prenatal mortality were extremely high. The field also struck me as complex. Unlike the previous rotations which were divided by units in the generality of the fields, surgery had five firms, medicine and obgyn had four. Pediatrics was divided into almost sections or department around diseases. So there was the malnutrition unit which was called A07, the diarrhea unit A06, the neonatalogy unit which was D block, the hematology and oncology unit (which was run by Prof Chifumbe Chintu- whom I had not met, but who was so renowned that I had heard of him in my secondary school days. One of my old class mates at Munali Victor Chisense, who had the peculiar habit of memorizing the lecture notes word by word, had a heart condition. He had recounted his experience of being seen by this famous Prof Chintu and being referred to the UK for a heart valve replacement. I recall thinking at the time, if there was this famous Zambian professor why did he not do the operation himself in Zambia. In retrospect Victor had suffered Rheumatic Heart disease, which is an autoimmune disease (a disease due to the body defense system mistakenly turning on itself) which damages the heart valve. Although quite classical of the superstition of the time, he told us he had stepped on some medicine which had been placed on the door way for his dad who was under secretary in one of the government ministries. He explained with conviction that this misfortune had caused his heart condition.He was the envy of the class except for the keloid (thickened scar)across his sternum(breast bone) which was a good deterrent.

There was the cardiology clinic which was run by Prof Mukelebai, who was also Dean of the Medical school. The student talk at the time was that he was not a fully qualified pediatrician, it was said he had only a diploma in pediatrics. I found him an excellent lecturer as well as extremely courteous to students. I later learnt that he was a diplomat of the American Board of Pediatrics, which basically meant he was fully trained in pediatrics. The use of the word diplomat may have been responsible for some of the misleading rumours in the school. He had a booming large voice which crackled when he talked. I never saw him in a white coat. He always hang a rather small stethoscope around his neck, which looked rather awkward for a large man. I wondered why he had not gotten one for his size. I learnt latter that this was a pediatric stethoscope, for children and babies. He was a cardiologist. So, I remember well his clinical tutorials on a child with a ventricular septal defect(a hole in the heart) and a condition called "Maladie d'Roger"- this is a small VSD that produces a loud murmur(heart sound caused by turbulent blood flow).

Lessons from my clinical rotations

I was so keen to get started with clinical medicine that I overlooked a couple of things. In the excitement of beginning to get into medical training, I had always looked to the hospital as the place where it would all happen. Having been a really good or top student in my basic science years, I was always expecting to do well in my clinical years. I was surprised when my performance declined a notch, from a general B/B+ grade I fell down to a C/C+ grade in the clinical years. My friend Elijah Chaila moved a notch up from his B/B+ grades to B+/A grades. This was a puzzle to me, because my enthusiasm in clinical medicine was not reflected in the results.

My father was a Human Resource Manager most of his life. He had firstly been a teacher as were many of his peers, when the opportunities opened up, he did Human Resource Training, in those days it had the less fancy name, of personnel management. He was good at his job and also gave all of us very good career advice. He dealt with people but he wasn't a people person, he was somewhat always uneasy with people. I had picked up some of this trait; I found it easier to deal with books than with people. This I reckoned was one of my greatest weaknesses in my clinical training. Medicine the career and Medicine the course both require good people skills. Show me a shy Doctor and I'll show you a Doctor that's struggling in medical practice. You need to be able to talk and think on your feet, to your colleagues, patients and teachers. This skill comes naturally to some and less so to others. I learnt that if I was to do well in medicine I had to become an actor, to pretend to be less shy than I was. This I determined to do, and over the years I have perfected it so well, that very few people can call me shy or timid.

During the period of my first clinical year, we also graduated in the preclinical sciences training. This was the peculiarity of the medical training of the time. It was a composite type of training, consisting of training in the medical sciences, which were a basis for training in the clinical sciences. So the first 4years of science training led to the award of the degree of Bachelor of Science in Human Biology. A poorly named qualification I would think with hindsight. In many other institutions with similar type of training if was called the Bachelor of Science in medical sciences, or in preclinical sciences. Nonetheless there was a great sense of achievement, among many of us, because after so many years of training, one finally had something to show for it. I was one of 7 of the top students in my class who graduated with a credit. We had no merits or distinction in the class. My friend Elijah Chaila, was top student, just falling few points shy of a merit. The other 5 guys were Ashraf Coovadia, Roy Chuunga, Sekelani Banda, Ajoy Chaabra and Joseph Yikona. Of the 7 only 2 of us have developed careers in medicine in Zambia. All the other 5 have over the years migrated overseas.

We graduated without much of the flare that characterizes graduations at the University of Zambia in these current times. There was also no induction ceremony, which was started, only later, in the 2000s. This has been a good addition to the medical graduation and involves the public reading of the Hippocratic Oath.

In 1989 I entered the intermediate clinical training year, which was called the 6th year of training. It was generally regarded as a leisurely year. In this period student spent clinical attachments in the major subspecialties of Surgery and Medicine in 2 of the terms. In the other 2 terms students were in Psychiatry for 9 weeks, and Community Medicine for another 9 weeks. There was no university examination at the end, but only a school examination. This was the period in which the cold war was at its peak. There was an organization called International Physicians for the Prevention of Nuclear War (IPPNW) which became popular at the time. There was a branch at the medical school, and I became an active member. We had the occasion to visit state house in 1988. Being the student leader at the time I read the speech to the first Zambian president Dr Kenneth Kaunda. It was my first experience of visiting State House and meeting the president close up. He was a towering figure over 1.8m in height with an aura of power around him. He was also an extremely humorous and civil man. The students group was called the Standing Committee for the prevention of nuclear war; a sponsored trip was planned to Hiroshima Japan in 1988. Unfortunately as fate would have it the whole class was asked to redo the surgical subspecialty exams, because of a high failure rate and a student appeal. I did not get to go. I remember, going in to see first the Assistant Dean, who directed me to see the Dean over this matter. In those days one rarely entered the Dean's office. So great was my desperation, that I gathered up the courage to see the Dean. The Dean at the time was Prof Kopano Mukelebai. He was a thoroughly nice man. The office was intimidating enough. I spent not more that 15minutes with the Dean and learnt from that quick encounter the character necessary for Deanship. Prof Mukelebai convinced me that I could not travel this time, but would have many opportunities to travel around the world in the coming years, but that this was not the right time to do so. Even though I was very unhappy, I was convinced of the veracity of his reasoning.

The Medical and Surgical attachments were so short that I barely recall the experience now. In surgery the specialties were so many that we barely spent 2 weeks in each. We spent few weeks each in Ear, Nose and throat unit. Which was called Otorhinolaryngoloy. It struck a chord because the demand for the services was so high and yet there was no Zambian specialist in the field. So for some time I entertained the thought of being an ENT surgeon. The other attachments were Facial Maxillary (bone surgery of the face and jaw) surgery, Ophthalmology (eye surgery), Anaesthesia (the field of how to prepare patients for operations) and Intensive Care. They all proved to be very interesting, however they were too short, to give sufficient understanding of the material. The medical specialties were much the same, we spent time in Radiology (the study of medical images including x rays) and Dermatology (diseases of the skin and sexually transmitted diseases). These rotations were treated with a much more casual attitude than the 5th year rotations, where attendance was rigorously enforced. The Psychiatry rotation was done at the specialist hospital in Chinama, which was a 200 bed facility. The facility was designed more like a sanatorium than a mental disease hospital. There was also a special unit where mentally ill patients who had committed serious offences were incarcerated. I found the field completely confusing. The disease patterns appeared poorly distinguished and blended into each other imperceptibly. The DSMB systems were just being developed and were extremely confusing. The professor of Psychiatry at the time, Prof Allan Haworth was well into his 70s, very hard of hearing, and taught mostly on alcoholism. Thus to my loss I learnt very little decent Psychiatry in my training. It was later to become clear what a big disadvantage I subsequently faced in attempting to do training in England with this deficiency. At the time being oblivious to this I was pleased to have completed and passed the rotation. Even then I noted the grave deficiencies in the health personnel levels in these specialties. Most of them were staffed by non physicians, with technician (college) level training called clinical officers.

I had always longed to travel, so between my 6th and 7th year, I had the opportunity to travel to Tanzania, through one of our student associations. I travelled with my class mate James Chipeta, one very nice Tumbuka Christian guy. We travelled by train to Muhimbira Medical center. We spent some time being hosted by the students at the University of Dar es Salaam Muhimbiri Medical College. The Tanzanias were well advanced in Medical training and already had a fully fledge Medical College with Dentistry and Pharmacy programmes. The people were very friendly; however the main language of communication was Swahili. So most students spoke English sparingly and with a great deal of unease. This was totally new to me. We travelled from Muhimbiri to Kenya the University of Nairobi, where the experience was totally different. The students were much more lively and more savvy. This showed me how politics can influence life in these two neighboring East African countries. The experience was a delightful one, and I had fond memories of the trip.

During my 6th year in medical training, my Christian life had blossomed. Three things happened at about this time. I joined the Kabwata Baptist Church, which was then meeting at the Kabwata Community Hall in Kabwata. The Church had recently commissioned a new pastor, called Conrad Mbewe.He had been the fiery chairman of the University of Zambia Christian fellowship in our years at the main campus, and was someone I knew well. He had gone up to Mufulira, after graduating at UNZA as a Mining Engineer. It was amazing to learn that he had then decided to stop his secular work and come to be the pastor of a small, then unknown church called Kabwata Baptist. His first sermon at the church as I recall, was from 1Corth 2:2, "I determined to know nothing among you except Jesus and him crucified". It was a text with a rich history. Dr Martyn Lloyd Jones, the famous English preacher, who had resigned his career as a Doctor, to become a pastor, had preached from this same text at his first church at Sandhurst in England.I must say the cinders still fly in my mind, when I recall the sermon.It was one of the best I had ever heard then or since.He had the uncannying ability to bring the full weight of his message to bear on the mind in such a way, that the sermon hit deep into a man's heart. I have attended Kabwata Baptist Church, since then, a period exceeding twenty five years.

The second was that I became the chairman of the Christian Fellowship group, called the Ridgeway Christian fellowship. It was a position I was reluctant to take.There were a modest number of medical students, who attended the group, close to 35. It was a closely knit group and we met regularly once a week.The immediate past Chairman was Simon Mphuka, who became the Director of the Churches Health Association of Zambia (CHAZ). We got support from a parachurch organizations, then called ZAFES(Zambia Fellowship of Evangelical Students). Our student liaison person, at the time was a devoted Christian man named Lazarous Phiri. He went on to study his PHD in Theology in the USA, and subsequently became the Principal of the Theological College of Central Africa(TCCA) in Ndola, one of the leading theological training centre for evangelical pastors in Zambia.

My third social experience at the time was becoming part of a small group of young career people, which quite by accident had confluenced around a guy called Eric Sinyangwe. Eric was then a teacher at David Kaunda secondary schools. He also had began to attend Kabwata Baptist Church a few years earlier than I had.We frequently walked home together from the Church services on Sunday morning, his house and the medical school campus being quite close to each other. Eric was a mild mannered guy with a most agreeable personality, this attracted friends to him, the way honey attracts bees.His house just behind the David Kaunda secondary school, which was shared with three other teachers, became a melting pot for this group of young career professionals, and was amusingly called the White House. The house was a two storey building previously occupied no doubt by the school principal, but had now fallen to some dereliction, it still had the remnants of its original white colour, and therefore was in fact white. It's stately appearance meant that ironically it looked rather like the White House. When I visted Washington DC and the Presidential residence the White House on Pennsylvania Avenue, the way tourists do, a few years later, I was amused to find a few similarities.

Eric was so giving a guy, that, a number of the young men, had inevitably used the house as a transit home until they found something of their own. Some of the guys I recall, were Buta Gondwe who became the Legal counsel for the Development Bank of Zambia, Patrick Chama who became Systems Manager for the United Nations, and now works in Lebanon and Charles Chilemu, who became the Business Manager at the USA embassy in Zambia. We ate together grew together and learnt about life together. It was a rich experience that strengthened me as a person and as a christain.I am thankful, to this day, for Eric and the White house.Eric, later, studied a Bachelors degree in English at the University of Zambia and is now the Headmaster of Chongwe Secondary School. I was the best man at his wedding a number of years later.

FINAL YEAR OF MEDICAL TRAINING

In 1990 I entered my final year of training. I could not believe that what appeared like endless years in school, I would complete my course and started working as a doctor. By this time I had develop some interest in a young lady who attend my church, Kabwata Baptist Church. Quite unintended. She was a beautiful rather demure young lady called Theresa Mutale. She was a Sunday school teacher at Kabwata Baptist Church, where I had began to attend church due to proximity to the school. Her brother, Mr Elias Mutale had at that time gone with his family to Canada for studies. He subsequently became a landed immigrant. So when we were just getting close Theresa left to join her brother in Canada.We wrote feverishly to each other over the 3 years or so, she was in Halifax. I can still remember the fragrance of her perfumed letters.The distance made it all the more clear that we were in love.The time for cell phones had not yet arrived, the process of e mails was still a dream at the time.So the relationship thrived on letters which came by post every 3 to 6months or so. I waited for the letters with a passion that could burst a man's heart. I poured over the letters obsessively, and kept them meticulously. It was an experience I had never had before.

The last year of medical training was like the junior year, we spent each of a 9 weeks' clinical rotation in Surgery, Medicine, Obstetrics &Gynaecology and Pediatrics.The novelty of Medicine had worn off a bit , and I had become less interested in some of the specialties as I horned into surgery sharpening my interest in the area. My rotations in surgery were never really enjoyable. I was unfortunate to spend both my senior and junior rotations in yellow firm. This was the Professorial firm. Unfortunately the unit paid little attention to student teaching. The unit focused on service outputs. The volume of work done by the unit was amazing. You sensed that the system was pervaded by a predominance of fear. The Doctors were all glittering and trying to avoid being shouted at. It was a mark of the time, where the Unit Consultant was a tyrant, and all the staff danced incessantly to his tune. When I look back now, it was remarkable that the firms were run in that manner. The Surgical rotation was rigid formal and lacked much teaching, in contrast, the Medical rotation was informal and completely disjointed. We learnt what we could from the young Senior House officers who were joining the units as postgraduate students. The pediatrics rotations were probably the best at the time. Even at the time the pediatrics department had two Professors, and Dr Shilalukey Ngoma had just returned from her studies in the United Kingdom with the MRCP degree (Membership of the Royal College of Pediatricians). In those days this qualification, was viewed as good as being a genius and having reached the pinnacle of your profession. All other post graduate masters were seen as inferior, in particular the local Masters of Medicine programme. This has changed somewhat over the years. The Obstetrics and Gynaecology rotation was less intimidating this time round. Mr Chikamata had left the headship, and a more relaxed approach to knowledge prevailed. I managed to pass all my courses and graduated in late October 1990.

In those days once the results were out within a month we were posted to 3 main hospitals to do internship. This is a one year pre registration year, in which the Medical Council as it was called then expected the graduate Doctor to spend a year of supervised work experience before getting full registration, and permission to practice independently. Postings were to Kitwe Central hospital, Ndola Central hospital and University Teaching hospital. Most people like me preferred to stay at UTH.

INTERNSHIP

Theresa returned from Canada, towards the end of 1990. I had finished Medical school and I was spending the holiday at my elder brother's place in longarces. He had recently transferred jobs from the mines to Zambia Airways then. Theresa and I spent lots of time together and our romance blossomed. Within a few months the Ministry of Health postings were out and I had been sent to the University Teaching Hospital in Lusaka, which was what I wanted. I moved into what was called interns block, which was a block between the medical block (E Block) within the hospital and the outpatient corridors. The block was 3 floors. The rooms were single rooms, intended for doctors on call, who needed to spend the night in the hospital. In the 1990s, the accommodation for Doctors was so difficult that they had all been turned into residences for doctors. I recall one of the Senior House officers (A Doctor who has been in practice for at least 2 years) who had two rooms and was living there with his family and children. So dire was the situation in those days that, I saw no problem with the room and was only happy to have a room of my own. Theresa and I spent lots of time together. During my internship years I began to learn how to drive. My Dad when he retired had left his last car a Fiat 132, with my elder brother Reynolds. His digs on Addis Ababa Drive, being not too far, I used to walk over and practice driving. Within a few months I was driving the car back and forth between my UTH flat and Northmead.

During my internship, three important things happened. I learnt how to drive, I applied to join the University as a staff development fellow and Theresa and I decided to get married. During the course of my training I had already made up my mind to become a Surgeon (Medical specialist who deals in treating people by operations). In those days the Zambian economy had began to decline. The local specialist training programmes had just started, but most people considered the training inferior to that obtained abroad. I had decided, being as ambitious as I was that I must obtain my surgical specialist training in the United Kingdom. So I decided I would join the University on its Staff

Development programme. This was a programme introduced in the 1960s, to train University lecturers. My plans, was by joining this programme to obtain a good quality specialist training. I had no particular interest in becoming a lecturer as such. My main interest was to get good quality specialist training. It turned out, off course, that I was naïve to imagine that things would be that simple. My primary interest was surgery, but I recognized that the interest of the University was more towards training people to teach in the basic science courses. Having had lectures by Mr Krikor (who latter became Professor and Head of Surgery at UTH), earlier, I recognized, immediately the link between Anatomy and Surgery. Therefore to my credit, I might say, I approached Prof Karashani (who became my mentor), to join the Anatomy department as an SDF. Prof Karashani was happy for me to join, but being an astute academic, he gave me a litany of the history of previous applicants for Anatomy training, both at his old University (the University of Dar–e-Salaam in Tanzania) and the University of Zambia. He told me about 2 previous SDFs whom the University of Zambia had sponsored to England who had not returned. On my part I was wise enough, or so I thought, not to reveal the full extent of my ambition in relation to the application. Thus the application was processed through the University bureaucracy while I continued my internship. I, off course, had a complete disdain for bureaucrats' and therefore for the University system altogether. I held the whole system in contempt. Nonetheless in my mind's eye, my intention was to run along with the system complete my training and then abandon the system altogether. This off course did not happen. Nor was this unusual, for a young man of my age in those times. There was a general feeling of the establishment, being politicized, regimented and lacking in both foresight innovation and intellect. Many young people of the time tried to distance themselves from the establishment which reeked of hollow political phrases and utopianism or so we thought at the time.

The internship itself was slave labour I found, with very little to learn except ones place in the medical hierarchy. This proved to be the lowest and a place of subservience. It was not at all what I had expected. I learnt to do my work keep my mouth shut and do what I was told. Many of our superiors relished the opportunity to put the young intern in his place. The medical knowledge of Medical school training was best packaged and recalled in later phases of the career I found. The consultant addressed all his questions to the Registrar (Mostly postgraduate trainees in that specialty) or at the very least to the Senior House Officer. The intern was a clerk, nothing more than a foot soldier who did what he was told and asked no questions. The more quickly you understood your position the better you got on with your superiors. I learnt that to challenge any of the seniors was to attract upon yourself the unmitigated fury of the medical establishment, it was taboo, and it was never done. My colleagues told me that this was less so in Kitwe and Ndola where doctors were fewer and no specialist post graduate programmes existed. The University Teaching Hospital was a like theatre stage and everyone liked to perform. The stuff taught in school and the stuff practiced in the wards was like 10 years apart. Medical practice, I found, suffered the dual curse of tradition and patronage it was an uneasy recipient of change. In one place I rotated at UTH the consultant never said hello to interns even in the corridor. He said to one of my colleagues I don't talk to interns. He was Head of his department!! I learnt that to be an intern was to be at the bottom of the rubbish heap, when things went great the consultants got the credit, when things went wrong the interns got all the blame. I was glad to survive internship, not everybody did, and many of my colleagues were made to repeat, frequently for what was viewed as insubordination. The formal reasons were couched in more academic language. It was an induction, into a militaristic and very traditional career. I discovered also that there was a lot of acrimony across specialties. The surgeons looked down upon the Obstetricians/Gynaecologist, the Internal Medicine Doctors (Adult Medicine specialists) despised the Surgeons and the Pediatricians (baby doctors) thought everybody else was incompetent. Sometimes all these specialist used the intern as a butting ram for their turf wars. I learnt to keep my head low and be polite to everyone. This was easy for me, because by nature I was a reticent person.

I don't recall having the time to pick up any book and read, let alone a medical book.My recollections is of being in a state of constant fatigue.

The lodging for the interns at the time was worse than the medical student rooms, certainly at the UTH. Sometime in the course of 1991, the pressure by the Resident Doctors Association.This was the "Union" so to speak for the junior doctors, and the more militant branch of the Zambia Medical Association, which was the parent association for all Doctors in Zambia. The RDA or ZMA pressure resulted in the government ceding off, Highland house to the Ministry of health for staff housing. Highland house was owned by the hostels board and was across the road from the UTH, across Independence Avenue. So many of the doctors in the interns block including me, moved to highland house. My room was on the 2nd floor of highland house. It was a single large room with a balcony and self contained bathroom and toilet. It was a lot better than my previous digs. During this period also there was a Doctors strike over wages.I recall a series of meetings with the then Permanent Secretary Dr Kawaye Kamanga, which resulted in the introduction of a special doctors allowance called the On call allowance. The salary of Doctors at the time was about 600 USD equivalent. The rate of the dollar to the kwacha had been fixed at about 2,500k to 1 USD.My gross salary at the time was about 1.5 million Kwacha.Subsquently this doubled with the addition of a fixed on call allowance to 1,200USD.This single act , to my mind has had a significant impact on the retention of Zambian doctors over the last 20 years.

The Medical Council of Zambia at the time also decided to change the format of the internship training. I discovered that internship training, which was an on job apprenticeship, was managed by the Ministry of Health and regulated by the Medical Council of Zambia. This of course was never taught to us in medical school. The training confined itself to disease processes with the exclusion of the medical profession and the health services in Zambia.Nobody can of course be blamed for this, because medical training was only a few years old in Zambia at the time. Now off course those managing Medical training appear to be sealing these types of deficiencies for current trainees. The duration was changed to 18 months, because of inadequacies in the skills of interns, who were being sent for a mandatory 2 years of rural, up country posting, and proving inadequate, especially in dealing with surgical emergencies. We were told that the total period would now be 18 months. The first 2 rotations could be selected by the individual Doctors as one 6month medical rotation followed by one surgical rotation. This meant one could rotate in Pediatrics and say Obstetrics and Gynaecology for the first year. The subsequent and final rotation could be a 6 month period in any of the 2 remaining specialties, either Internal Medicine or Surgery. This single decision proved to be my undoing when I tried to do surgical training in Ireland in Dublin 11 years later in 2001. The rotations that had been done by our predecessors had been for a period of one year, 3 months in each of the 4 main specialties.

My first attachment was to Obstetrics and Gynaecology; I was displeased to find that I actually had no choice in the selection of internship rotations. The UTH management simply posted us by a rota system oblivious of any personal preferences. I would much rather have done Surgery and Internal Medicine in the first one year of internship. Therefore I ended up doing internship in Obstetrics and Gynaecology and Internal Medicine. In the republic of Ireland, the internship has to be done for a period of 6months in each of Surgery and Internal Medicine, anything else was considered incomplete internship training. The Medical Council of Ireland, considered Obstetrics and Gynaecology a subspecialty of Surgery and Pediatrics a subspecialty of Internal Medicine. This proved an insurmountable problem for me later.

Internship in Obs & Gyn was an experience; it was a minefield for a young intern. One found that there were myriads of potential pitfalls for the uninitiated, which I proved to be. The unit to which I was attached divided itself into a Gynae team and an Obs team. We were two interns in the unit. After 3 months we swopped. I started in the Gynae unit. The gynae unit had a small minor procedure room in C01 ward with transit admission facilities, and our admission ward was C02. We were on call every 3rd day, because in those days there were a total of 4 firms in the department. There were two postgraduate students in our unit Dr Reuben Mbewe (who later became Director of Public Health at the Ministry of Health) and Dr Velepi Mtonga(She later rose to become

Permanent Secretary in the Ministry of Health and subsequently Personnel Service Management Division at Cabinet Office). They were good Doctors and worked excellently well together. The call days were heavy and exhausting. Manual Vacuum extraction (MVE) had just been introduced for patients with incomplete abortions. Incomplete Abortions are pregnancies less than 28weeks which had being partially lost or expelled. These patients often came to the hospital with vaginal bleeding. The guidelines were that only early incomplete abortions could be treated by MVE as it was called, those less than 8 weeks. So after seeing a whole load of 50 patients in a day, one lined up 8 to 10, 16 year old girls with incomplete abortions for MVEs. I was naïve to think that everything was on the straight and narrow. It struck me that the numbers were too many, and lots of people took a keen interest in the MVE room. Over the first few months I learnt the subtleties of Obstetrics and Gyneacological practices. A number of "Apparent Abortions" were initiated at private clinics in the city and sent for completion in the hospital. The young teenage girls were coached on what to say to the uninitiated intern, who would inadvertently complete an in fact criminal abortion. In one of these instances I was working on a young teenage girl in the MVE room when I felt something hard inside the uterus. To my complete astonishment I pulled out a stick which had been poked into the uterus. Gynaecology proved to be an education in the vices of men and women. The corridors of the C01 were littered with people intent on burying, the ills of their children, nieces, nephews and girl friends in the disposable bins of the hospital. There was also money to be made by those shrewder then I was, among the desperate parents, teenagers, school officials and police officers. I became sure then that those heavy responsibilities should have been given to more experienced and seasoned doctors. However such was the shortage of doctors in those days that every hand was required on deck, the interns had to survive the night and manage in the best way they could. The MVE procedure was a nasty one. The young girls were given no pain killers; the uterus was curetted with a large suction syringe until it was empty. The nurses who assisted in the theatre room seemed to take pleasure in scolding, the often frightened, teenagers over their illicit sexual activities. No thought was given, by the nurses, that some maybe genuine cases of natural incomplete abortions in a young married woman. Though admittedly, even I saw that these were few and far between. Many overly enthusiastic interns perforated the uterus in the process of the MVE, with often devastating consequences. The MVE theatre decongested the main theatre, and reduced the work for the postgraduate students and the unit, so in spite of its short comings; it was well approved off, in the department. After each call day the firm on duty and the incoming firm did a hand over round. The process took at least 2 hours. We would start in the labour ward and end down in the gynae ward. The combination of two units meant that there were close to 10 Doctors in attendance. This trail of Doctors breezed through the two admission areas at break neck speed. The unit interns had to present all the cases concisely and quickly. It was an unnerving experience. One had to assimilate the history of the case, the diagnosis, the management and the plan for the case. Often times the diagnosis was challenged and you had to defend diagnosis with a sufficient measure of humility. It was a difficult thing to pull off always. Some diagnoses were difficult, and sometimes the unit was spread thin, there was no time to cross check with the Registrar (the postgraduate doctor) on duty. So you got it wrong, and were devoured by both the incoming unit and your own unit. It was an emotionally exhausting experience. The most humiliating question, you would get asked was, where were you trained? This question implied that you were not properly trained. My worst experience which happened twice was to mistake an ectopic pregnancy for a threatened abortion. In a pressure intense setting of the gynae filter it was not unusual to miss the diagnosis. The history was taken at a dizzy speed, the opportunity to recheck the history and examine the patients once stashed in the poorly lit wards and crevices of C01 ward were nil. That had me almost killed!! I learnt, to my loss that both cases gave history of bleeding with pain at about 6 to 8 weeks of pregnancy. The subtlety, lay in the nature of pain and the bleeding. In ectopic pregnancy the bleeding precedes the pain, while the opposite is true of threatened abortion. The nature of the bleeding is also different in ectopics, there are drops of dark old blood, while in threatened abortion the blood is bright, fresh blood in larger volumes. In the later the treatment is conservative in the former the treatment is emergency surgery. So it's understandable that I almost got myself killed by my unit.

When my rotation in gynae was complete I washed my hands and thanked heaven. However I learnt in Obstetrics that I had jumped from the frying pan into the fire. I learnt that while in Gynae you needed to be sure of what you were doing within hours, in Obstetrics you had to do it within minutes. While in gynae you sat in one lice infested chair and had patients came to you in turn. In obstetrics, you run from room to room, to attend to myriads of Obstetric emergencies falling over each other for your attention. You rarely could sit on any chair at all. If the clinical diagnosis was difficult in Gynae the management in Obstetrics was a minefield. Not only was it difficult because I lacked experience, but also because the consultants had varied opinions on the management of different Obstetric patients. The Midwives (nurses dealing with normal deliveries in the labour ward) I discovered, knew more obstetrics than I did. So when a midwife phoned and said, there was a problem, you knew pretty well that it was a big problem. My consultant in Internal Medicine, always said, when you are not sure what to do, ask the nurses. I took this advice liberally and it helped me survive labour ward.

The Obstetric section like the Gynae section had two key areas, the labour ward where pregnant women did deliveries and the Obstetric ward. The Obstetric ward was where women were admitted because they had other diseases of pregnancy or they were not yet in labour (the process when the baby starts moving down the birth passage until it comes out). Every week there was one obstetric outpatient clinic and one gynae outpatient clinic. The two clinics were somewhat confusing and difficult for me. Eventually I released that the main thing that was done in the clinics was to evaluate which patient needed operations and which ones did not. The patient load was always high and there was really none to supervise the intern. So one made one's own luck as best as one could. I found that the main Gynae problem was infertility (failure to have children). The key investigation was to determine the patency of the tubes by Hysterosalphingography. This rather fancy name was just an x ray test in which a dye was passed through the female reproductive tubes (The fallopian tubes) to see if they were open or not. Many women believed this test alone could make them have a child because it opened up the blocked tubes. It did some times work. In Obstetrics on the other hand the main issues was to determine which patient should have an elective Caesarian Section (which patient should have the baby removed by operation) and which one should be allowed to go in to labour. Among the consultants there was no unanimity on this. Similarly in the labour ward the key decision was which patient should be allowed to go through labour and which one should have an emergency Caesarian Section. The word Caesarian I learnt came from the belief that Julius Caesar the emperor of Rome had being delivered by an operation.

The department held a Maternal Mortality Meeting every once a month at which the cocks came home to roost. Fortunately the intern was never centre stage; therefore it was an excellent place to learn obstetrics. The consultant roasted the Registrar (the trainees in Obstetrics and Gynaecology), it wasn't pleasant, but it was fun to watch. I learnt some dos' and don'ts' that kept me afloat in the murky waters of obstetrics.

So unpredictable and uncertain did I find Obstetric and Gynaecology, that I was relieved to finish the rotation and enter the much safer field of Internal Medicine.

I began my second 6 months rotation in the department of Internal Medicine (Adult Medicine) about March 1991. My consultant was Professor Joseph M Pobee. He was the Head of department as well as the Head of Unit 2. Prof Pobee was a brilliant physician and an excellent teacher. He was from Ghana, and had come to Zambia under a World Health Organisation supported exchange programme, or so it was rumoured. Like most men of brilliance he was temperamental and also clearly favored young women students or doctors. He was less lenient on young men like me. His mood swings were legendary, and the first thing one did before going into his office was to get the ok nod from his secretary. If the ok nod was not given, you entered at your own risk. His unit had a second consultant. It was rumoured that he had made many unsuccessful attempts at the postgraduate specialist examination the MRCP (Membership of the Royal College of Physicians). He eventually past the local post graduate examination the Master of Medicine degree in Internal Medicine. He was perhaps for this reason somewhat belligerent and acrimonious. There were more or less two units within unit 2, as I later found. The consultant and his team worked the female ward, while in general Prof Pobee and his team worked the male side. The consultant had a clever registrar at the time called Dr Mudenda. The two got on like a house on fire. She tended to moderate some of his excesses, I found. Medicine was a busy department. In those days the HIV epidemic had reached its peak and we saw the effect in the hospitals. The call days were always busy with over 100 admissions and deaths exceeding 10-15%. The medical admission ward was like a war zone. There were floor beds wherever space was available. In the course of my internship, we had a number of postgraduate students studying their Master of Medicine degree in adult Medicine join our unit. One whom I recall was Dr Joseph S Banda. He was an army doctor and was Major at the time. He was a sober serious and hard working doctor. He later became Director of Medical services and a Brigadier General in the Medical Corp of the Zambia Defence Forces. He was a particular favourite of the Professor. No mean achievement I can tell you.

My Adult Medicine was fair and I developed reasonable clinical skills. One interesting case I had was case brought in by a local General Practioneer (A Doctor working in his own private clinic) in town. This young girl had suddenly developed facial and body spasms. What I later learnt were extrapyramidal side effects of Plasil (an antiemetic drug-used to suppress vomiting).She was unable to speak, had neck extension and trismus (spasms of the jaw muscle –the masseter muscle). I recall this case because I was completely unsure what to do. One of the senior House officers on my team, made the diagnosis of drug induce dystonia.The basic treatment was muscle relaxation and waiting it out. It was also advised to use an antidystonia medicine called Artane.The girl recovered well and was discharged after a day or two.

Before my internship was completed Prof Pobee invited us to his house at the University of Zambia Canada court as it was called.It was within the premises of the main University of Zambia on Great East

Road. We had a lot of fun. He was jovial and had along over 10 to 15 doctors. In those days, when economic times where hard, there was the appearances of affluence in the home. Prof Pobee lived alone, his wife it was said was a Professor of Medicine and had stayed in Ghana. His children were all grown and some where Medical doctors in the US. My internship ended about October 1991.

While my documents to join the SDF (Staff development Programme) in Anatomy were being processed by the University, I spent 1 month in General surgery. During that brief period, I worked in Green Firm with Mr Girash Desai, who later became Professor of Surgery. Since I had a great love for surgery, I enjoyed my work there, though it was short lived. Even in those days Mr Desai was rather eccentric. He would come onto the surgical admission ward and say "any problems Bowa". He would do that regularly three to four times in the day, and then say take my blood pressure. It was most amusing.

Getting Married

The paper work was all done by December 1991 and I joined the University of Zambia as a Staff Development Fellow in the department of Anatomy in the School of Medicine.

My girlfriend Theresa Mutale had returned from Canada, a year earlier and our romance had blossomed. Her birthday was on the 19th of December and we planned to get married on the 14th December 1991.The times were uncertain, because this was an election year and there was a great wind of change from a one party state towards democracy. Everybody was uncertain what democracy would bring, but there was a hunkering for change. The old politics of suppression and dominance of one party communist style politics had left a bitter taste of poverty and lack of innovation.There was a sense of change in the air. Everybody was gripped with the frenzy of the time. We felt that it was a good time to get married given the uncertainty of the time. We got married a few days before the elections of 1991. The wedding was a plush affair for the time.It was held at the American Dome within the Showgrounds in Lusaka. We spent our honey moon at Fairview Hotel in Fairview Lusaka.Theresa and I lived for a while at High Rise Flats opposite the University Teaching Hospital. We eventually moved to a bed sit at Marshlands as we fully moved from the Ministry of Health to the University.Theresa worked for a project on the Environment in the Biology department at UNZA, this move proved quite convenient. The project was managed by Mr Douglas Kunda one of our church mates at our local church Kabwata Baptist Church.Through this project the Environmental Council of Zambia was formed by an Act of Parliament and she and Mr Kunda were some of the first staff of the Environmental Council of Zambia in 1993, now called ZEMA (Zambia Environmental Management Agency).Dr Kunda eventually obtained a PHD in Computer Sciences and now works for Mulungushi University in Kabwe.

We had many friends who like us were beginning their careers as lecturers, in the various schools in the University. In those days the

University of Zambia pursued a vigorous training programme for developing teaching staff. All these lecturers to be were housed at Marshlands. Marshlands is a University Guest House located opposite the University of Zambia Great East Road Campus. It is appropriately named because it is a rather swampy and water logged area. It had a small dining area and close to 50 rooms of varying sizes. From single type rooms to bed sits. It was a transit house for staff returning from training abroad or those designated for training as lecturers. We made many friends there and had regular get togethers and parties.

We made great friendships. One of the greatest challenges I faced was getting to work every morning. The School of Medicine campus at Ridgeway was a good 30 minutes drive from our Marshlands residences. The bus routes were so convoluted that I could hardly get to work on time. Occassionally I used the UNZA staff bus which took other people working at the Medical school from the main campus. The SDFs salaries were quite low and it was not possible to buy a car immediately. I had learnt how to drive using my father's old car the previous year, during my internship. So initially we used the old fiat 132 until we eventually sold it off. With the sale I bought my first car from Prof Oliver Saasa, who had been the director of the Institute of Social and economic Research, which was located in Munali. It was a somewhat run down Datsun 120y. Theresa was somewhat displeased. It required a lot of mechanical work and was a constant drain on our meager income. It helped somewhat to relieve my perpetual transport difficulty to and from work.

There were two of us in the Anatomy training programme at the time. Sekelani Banda who had been my class mate in Medical school joined about a month or two after me. He had done his internship at Ndola Central Hospital. We spent time as tutors and demonstrators to the Medical Students in the Anatomy course. It was pleasant work, and I became very conversant with the key branches of Anatomy. We spent time with Professor Karashani, who mentored us and supervised our work. The Assistant Dean in charge of postgraduate training at the time was Prof Antoinelle Bagshawe, a rather brush Australian female Professor who was responsible to facilitate the overseas training of

SDFs. With the help of the Overseas Development Agency (ODA) under the British Government we both obtained scholarships to study for the Master of Science degree in Anatomy at the University of Glasgow in Scotland.

UNIVERSITY OF GLASGOW

The British Council office in Lusaka made all the necessary arrangements for travel as well as admissions to the University of Glasgow in Scotland. They also arranged for a pre travel orientation, which allowed us to meet Zambian students who had studied in the United Kingdom. It was useful and gave some sneak preview of what to expect.

I arrived in England in October 1991, having travelled only sparingly before then; I was impressed with what I saw in London. The country was beautiful; everything was green, and meticulously organized. I landed at Heathrow Airport and was assisted by a British Council official who received me and helped to make, what than looked like are rather complex connecting flight to Glasgow Airport in Scotland. It had not occurred to me then that there was a distinct difference between Scotland and England.The Glasgow Airport was a more modest place, and when I tried to get a taxi to Glasgow University, I struggled to understand the cab man. The Scotsmen in Strathclyde had a very broad accent which was a trade mark of the Glaswegian accent.The local Scottish language was Gaelic which accounts for the accent. Strathclyde was the Gaelic word, meaning in the valley of the Clyde. The Clyde was the main river in Scotland. Strathclyde was one of the 9 provinces of Scotland at the time, who's main city was Glasgow.

I settled into the postgraduate housing a comfortable walking distance from the University. The University of Glasgow was the second oldest University in Scotland after St Andrews University in Fife on the East Coast of Scotland. Glasgow was the largest commercial city and was on the west Coast of Scotland. It had a reputation akeen to The University of Cambridge or Oxford; it was the Ivy League equivalent in Scotland. The school was established in 1451 and this is proudly displayed in the front gate of the old building of the main school. The motto of the University which stood boldly at the gates was "Via Verita Vita" is Latin for the "The way, the truth and the Life" .The University had renown through many famous alumni including Adam Smith the father of modern economic- the Adam Smith building was across the road from the main building of the University , Joseph Lister the famous inventor of medical antispesis,the chemist Joseph Black, the engineer James Watt and off course William Hunter the Anatomist.The Hunterian Museum a large collection of Anatomy specimens was bequeathed to the University by the Hunters, and was located in the Anatomy department as I discovered.

The Anatomy building was through the old part of the University Gates off the Kelvingrove road which was the main street through the University. Having only being to the University of Zambia, which was located in a distinct walled off site, I found the diffusely placed University rather strange.The University blended with the town imperceptibly, and it was often difficult to distinguish what was part of the University and what was part of the town.Within a few days I had settled in the department of Anatomy. The Head of Department was Dr Tony Payne who later became Professor, I was surprised to learn that he was a Professor of Zoology(The study of Animals). Our course co-ordinator was a rather eccentric bachelor called Dr John Shaw-Dunn. He came from a distinguished line of Medics, his father was Professor of Pathology at Glasgow University and his brother was Professor of Psychiatry. His head was almost completely bald, but he frequently stroked the last threads of hair in a most academic manner. His accent was distinctly English though he was fiercely loyal to Scotland. His favourite joke was his elder sister's frequently chide, "John behave yourself or I'll put formalin in your tea and that will fix you". Formalin is the chemical preservative used on human bodies to keep them from rotting and allows for their use in student teaching on human organs. John Shaw-Dunn to my surprise did not know how to drive a car.He got to work on the bus. Several of the other lecturers rode bicycles. The beautiful SAAB in the car park of the department belonged to the secretary to the head of department. Notwithstanding his eccentricities, John Shaw –Dunn was the most intelligent Anatomist I have ever met. Not only did he have a thorough knowledge of Anatomy, but he understood the science off it. When I later met the president of the Royal College of Surgeons of Glasgow in New Orleans ,Prof Teasdale (who together with Jennet, described the Glasgow Coma scale not far from the University at the Southern General hospital in Glasgow),and I told him , I had studied in Glasgow, he spoke very highly of John Shaw-Dunn.

I learnt later that the Professor of Anatomy, who was one of the editors of the famous Cunningham's Textbook of Anatomy, had recently retired. To our good fortune as we learnt from our predecessors, he apparently was particularly racist. Though the Anatomy department had a great history, the Masters programme in Anatomy was poorly designed. It had been structured for training of overseas Doctors who would become lecturers in their home countries in Anatomy. One Zambian trainee had gone through the programme and one more was in his second year, when we arrived. Sekelani and I would make it four Zambian trainees in Anatomy at the University. The first was Dr Boyd Mudenda who I later met in 1995 in Zambia. He went on to study surgery. Prof Karashani never ceased to decry this loss to us all endlessly. Elliot Kafumache was two years our senior at medical school, he was already doing his research on nerve related trauma with a rather ingenious supervisor, who had, some rather poor teaching skills, called Dr Bill Maxwell, by the time we arrived.

The office I had been given had previously belonged to a Nigerian PHD student called Mike Badawale, he had pinned up a verse of scripture which was most instructive "Don't be discouraged or lose heart, be courageous and strong – for I will see to it that everything is completed correctly" from 1Chronicles chapter 28 verse 20. The quote was from the living bible. I met Mike two years later and when I heard his story, I was greatly enriched. He spent 5 years in the department. His commonwealth scholarship was for 3 years. He run out of money and his sponsors abandoned him. He was a destitute in Scotland, but persevered until he completed his PHD. His supervisor was the head of department. When he first arrived, the departmental secretary warned him, that whoever had sent him to study at the University of Glasgow had made a grave mistake. Though he came with a Masters degree in Anatomy, he was made to redo the Masters degree, before starting his PHD programme. Fortunately for us our stay in Glasgow was much more pleasant. I determined to make the most of the opportunity and do all that I was ambitious to do. My ambition at the time, somewhat misplaced, I might add, was to obtain a PHD in Anatomy and the FRCS qualification from the Royal College of Surgeons of England. It was naïve and probably ill advised, however I was 26 years old and the scholarship had given me an opportunity which I was going to use to the full extent possible.

My digs as the college residences were called, was a large block of four floors, each apartment housing 4 postgraduate students. The apartments had 4 bedrooms, two shared bathrooms and one TV room, come kitchenette. One of my apartment mates, was from Jordan. He was reading for a PHD (Doctorate degree) in Business Administration. He was over 1metre 90cm. He was probably not more than 20 years old. His English was good, though heavily accented. He was a curious fellow and somewhat self consumed. He had this completely misguided impression that they were hordes of Scottish women pursuing his affections even though none of them had said so. The University had a large indoor sports facility and he frequently went there for a swim. He would come back and let me know that the Scottish women really fancied him. When I enquired how he had arrived at this conclusion, he would say they way they looked at him. I thought that this was probably quite naïve of him and I suggested he have a chat with some of them and see whether this was in fact the case. He ignored this and instead tried to argue that the way a woman looks at you is sufficient proof of this. Having never heard anything like this before I was completely baffled. It occurred to me later that coming from a restricted social life in a predominantly Arab country, access to women was severely limited. Perhaps also as eye contact between men and women was generally frowned upon, the western free male female interaction could have been a cause of confusion for him.

Other than this we got on pretty well. I learnt from him that his parents sponsored him to study in Glasgow, and that it was considered highly beneficial to have a PHD from overseas in general, but particularly in the United Kingdom. He was surprised that I was being sponsored for my studies through British government support, as was I that his family could support his training with their own finances. The University fees for overseas students at the time were close to 8,000 pounds per year. There were a least three other Zambian students in the Business school who were studying in Glasgow with me at the time. Two of whom I got to know reasonably well. My first few weeks in the University was spent getting my bearings right and learning the ropes. I quickly understood that I would need to work on my computer literacy. Throughout my medical training I had never had access to a computer and I had no idea how to use one. The thought of sitting in front of one was extremely frightening. However most things were computerized and so there was no getting round it. Unfortunately it was generally assumed that all the students were computer friendly, so throughout the orientation period one was constantly receiving written instruction about access to various university services for post graduate students which included terms like log in and log out domain name etc. I avoided these things as much as I could. However for key services this was not possible.

I needed to open a bank account, there was a branch of the Clydesdale bank on the campus (The Clydesdale bank was one of the major Scottish banks at the time), in order to get my monthly stipend from the British Council. I needed to get a library card and as my wife was sending me messages by e mail (which up to then I had not understood the value off), I needed access to the computer room. Initially someone printed out e mail messages for me and I found them in my pigeon box (the postgraduate designated mail box). However they were getting tired of this, and besides I had to respond to my wife's mail sooner or later. The bank was a necessary ordeal and armed with a list of instructions from my British Council minder I approached the Clydesdale bank with caution. The first attempt was aborted, I took one look at the orderly queues at the 3 or so counters and felt I would embarrass myself in front of the Scottish students. Finally after 3 attempts I got up to the counter, the process was less intimidating than it appeared, a friendly red haired bank clerk smiled and asked me to enter my "pin". I off course not knowing what my pin was entered by computer number which was 8 digits long. The cashier gave me a quizzical look, and said simply "It is too long". I quickly keyed in the next number that came to mind, which was a 4 digit number that had come with instructions from the bank. The clerk smiled and said, how much do you want. I was taken aback, a little, because back home in Zambia, there are forms to fill in the bank, before you got your money out. I recovered quickly enough, to receive my first 50 pound Scottish note. The bank was plain sailing after that.

My next hurdle was the ATM- Automatic teller machine. To start with I simply avoided using the machine at all costs. Then one day while in the Clydesdale bank a few streets from the central campus branch. The teller there asked me why I don't use the ATM, because there was a charge for using the counter for my transactions each time. So I gave myself the task of learning to use the ATM machine. Coming from Africa at a time when such machines were unheard off, it proved intimidating. Nowadays, off course, these machine are littered up and down many African countries including Zambia, however back then, money coming out of a hole in the wall, would have been considered pretty advanced. So I spent some evenings pretending to be window shopping in the area near the bank, when in fact I was gathering information about this "ATM" machine. Eventually on one quite night I went up to the machine, it was basically a little TV screen, with a dialing component of the phone below it and a money slot area. The machines were more basic than they are now and had blood coloured words on the screen.The first approach was designed to gather information. So only after the third or fourth approach did I attempt anything. It took one or two attempts to get the sequence right and get out some money. After that the bank part was a stroll in the park. My next big hurdle was the computer centre. I used the exact same approach. Eventually I went into the computer room; spoke to the person on the desk who directed me to student advisors. I concluded later that all these people assumed I was computer literate. What I got was a piece of paper with a user name and pass word and couple of sheets of paper about rules and regulations for usage of the computer room. When I had worked my way through these materials, I realized that in fact all I had now was permission to use the computer room, while, what I had been looking for were the skills to use the computer services. This clearly was a different matter and the student advisors took it for granted that I had the skills already. Being somewhat timid, as one is in a new environment, and not wishing to attract attention to myself, I decided to correct this deficiency myself. So armed with the user name and password I went to the computer room again. After a number of attempts I got access to the computer services. Gradually by trial and error I began to use the E mail services and kept in touch with home. It was an experience that required quite a bit of courage.

When I joined the University I set my goal to be the best Surgeon I could and the University would be the transit vehicle towards this goal. When I got to Glasgow University I found the academic life of the lecturers in the Anatomy department appealing. I modified my goal to that of becoming a Professor of Surgery. The University of Glasgow was the first step along this route I took it. So soon after arriving in Glasgow I made an ambitious plan of achieving as much as I could on the scholarship I had been given. The scholarship was for two years. I set about preparing myself to do at least 3 things. These were to complete the Masters degree in Anatomy, to sit and pass the first part of the examination of the Royal college of Surgeons, which was the first part towards Surgical Specialist training in the United Kingdom and to sit the registration examinations for the UK, this would allow me to continue my surgical training after completion of the Masters degree in Anatomy. It was an ambitious plan which almost worked. In addition I decided to sit the registration examinations for the USA, which would give me the option to obtain surgical residency (post graduate specialist training) in the USA. The first thing I discovered was all these ambitions required money. My stipend from the scholarship was no more than 650pound. This was not a lot of money by any standard. The University employed all the post graduate students as tutors, which allowed for a small additional income of no more than a 100 pounds a month. Many of my friends having more financial ambitions took on odd jobs to raise money. For me this would be impossible, because as it was I had barely enough time to do my Masters training material study as well as study for all the other 3 additional examinations I had elected to take on. So I had to reduce my expenses. I tried as much as I could to use the library resources of the University and not buy any books I did not need to.

By the end of my first year, I had sat and passed the part 1 examinations, of the Royal College of Surgeons of England. I had also passed the Education Commission for Foreign Medical graduates (ECFMG) exams in Edinburgh. This examination was for admission into residency training in the USA. I had attempted and not passed the PLAB examination which was the registration examination to work in the UK. I had only barely failed the oral exam, but had passed the written exams.

My wife, Theresa came to the UK to join me within about 3 months of my arrival in England.I picked her up in London at Heathrow Airport and we went by train to Glasgow. In those days the journey was almost 12hours.The speed of the trains have increased since then and it takes a much shorter time. The reunion was intense and emotional. We slept on each other's laps as we travelled to Glasgow. I had moved into a larger apartment close to the University, because the University quarters did not allow for married couples. The apartment was rather small and Theresa always complained of being cold and lonely. We moved to a council flat which was a two bed roomed flat, cost less and allowed Theresa a lot more domestic freedom. She had the fun of doing up the rooms, working in the kitchen and all the things I learnt women love to do to the home. We also had the advantage of a least 3 Zambian families in the same area. The place was called Sight hill and we lived in Fountain hill. The area was said to be unsafe and ridden with crime. However by African standard it was a quiet and peaceful neighbourhood. There was a Presbyterian church nearby and Theresa and I attended services there. The minister was Rev Jones, we got to know him and some of the congregation quite well. We had initially been going to a famous church in the centre of town called the Tron.Saint Georges Tron, in Mandela square in the centre of Glagsow.The pastor there was called Sinclair B Ferguson, he was a world renowned pastor and had written many Christian books.

Our first born daughter was born in Glasgow at the Queen Mother Maternity Hospital. We called her Lesa Wachikuku which means God is merciful. We had decided firstly to give all our children African names. Secondly we decided to name them in keeping with the circumstances of their birth and as token of thank you to God, who had given them to us. This was in keeping with the biblical practice as we understood it. Chiku, as we called her for short, was quite a handful to start with. She had lots of colic (baby abdominal cramps) and kept Theresa and I awake all night. Chiku was born on the 27th September 1993.Theresa had an unpleasant experience over the period, she had been sickly, home sick and tired most of the time. Our flat was on the 19th floor of the sighthill flats.It had a good view but the lifts only went up to the 18th floor. We had to climb an additional 1 floor of stairs. It was our first time as a couple to really live in a proper house and it was great fun.In the course of Theresa's pregnancy we had to go to the hospital because she had a lot of vomiting and nausea.

On the day of delivery, Theresa woke up at about 11:00, with mild abdominal pain, and said her waters had broken. I called an ambulance and we had her taken to the Royal Maternity hospital about 15minutes drive from our residences. She had very little labour pain. However it turned out the baby was mildly malpositioned. The baby was not fully flexed in the tummy. The doctor in charge Dr Pringle had her given an epidural (jab in the back to control pain) and the baby was delivered by forceps. Theresa stayed about 3 days in the hospital.

In the second year of our stay in Glasgow, I had finished most of my examination and was struggling to arrange my posting in order to complete a PHD degree as well as the fellowship examinations in surgery. I got a promising job offer in Dundee for a tutorship, which eventually failed to materialize. The year was also busy with preparation for my research work and defense of my dissertation. After my first year examination which was a general Anatomy examination, in which we had written examinations in all the main branches of Anatomy, I proceeded to the second part of the course which was research. By this time I had settled very well in Glasgow and was quite used to the key parts of the city. Travel between home and the University took about thirty minutes. I had learnt the quickest travel routes and bus numbers. It was unnerving at first but I got used to it, with time. In my research year I was supervised by Dr Rob Smith, he was Senior Lecturer in Anatomy. He was a Zoologist trained at

Cambridge. He was English and so I had no difficulty in understanding him. My research was in the cytology of Dorsal Root Ganglia cells (studying the sensory nerves cells of mice) response to mercury. Mercury is a chemical substance which is used in many industries, but is known to damage nerve cells. It was interesting work and involved the acquisition of several skills. These included the dissection of dorsal root ganglion cells from mice. Placing the cells in culture, which was a special media in where the cells could grow. The cell plates were place in a special incubator with a regulated appropriate temperature. These cells were examined under a special microscopy called the transmission electron microscopy (Special microscope for seeing cells in culture). The Scanning Electron Microscope was another special microscope which was used. This microscope made the images of the cells very large and allowed the surface features of the cells to be seen. Using these two means any damage to the inner or outer cells was easily seen. Graduated increasing doses of mercury were used to see their effects on cultured cells. It was interesting work. There were 2 other researchers in Dr Smith's lab at the time. There was a Chinese PHD student who was extremely intelligent called Dr Zhang. He, however, spoke very little English; though to my surprise his written English was excellent. The second guy was a BSc honours student who was Asian British and a little cocky. They were pretty nice guys who were also working with DRG cells with different in vivo toxins. Dr Zhang got a post doc position in the USA and latter moved to the USA.

Our social life was limited both by my time and the small circle of friends we had. There were a number of Zambian families in Glasgow, at the time and we got together for some social functions. My friend Sekelani Banda and his family were our neighbours at Fountainwell in Sighthill. Several other Zambian were also studying at the University at the time and we had a few good social gatherings. The tragic death of the Zambia football team over the coast of Gabon occurred about this time. There was a great sense of gloom among the group. The makeshift team that took part in the Confederation of Africa Football (CAF) cup at the time performed much better than had been expected reaching the semi finals and losing to Nigeria. I realized then that tragedy at home has a 10 fold impact when you are abroad. It has an isolating and devasting impact. Especially with there being so little news, particularly in those days when social media was only just developing.

I finished my research and completed my dissertation in about July 1994.My examiner was a professor from Dundee. He and Prof Tony Payne the head of Department were my examiners. My defense was good hearted and I knew that I had passed before the exam ended. I had applied for a lectureship in Jamaica, which was showing promise. It was unclear if I might get a post in Jamaica so my wife Theresa and my daughter Chiku went on a head back to Zambia in August 1994.I stayed for a few month to complete all my formalities. I returned to Zambia in October 1994.The job in Jamaica did not materialise.

MARSHLANDS

Having been away from Zambia for 2 years continuously, I was amazed at how the country had changed. The infrastructure was much more dilapidated than I recalled. This may have been due to the upgrade of environment that I had been exposed to for the last 2years. Most striking was the increase in street vending which was before this unheard of. The kind of disorderly street vending that makes you hold your pockets very tightly. The streets were choked with people selling all types of merchandise. It reminded me of my visit to Tanzania in the 1980s.The country had clearly suffered the impact of sudden withdrawal of government social subsides. It was clear that no one had anticipated the results. When the 2nd republic came in 1990, I think everyone felt it was the dawn of better economic times. This I think was wishful thinking.

What struck me most as we struggled to find our feet and some accommodation from the university, was the development of a middle class. There were actually some among our peers who bought and owned houses. Our local church, which we started to attend again, was the clearest sign of this. Several of our friends whom we had left in rented accommodation were now living in their own houses. The credit market had clearly come to Zambia and those in formal employment were benefitting from it. We got accommodation at Marshlands, much the same as we had had before leaving. We had a small single flat actually a bed sit. Theresa started work again at the Environmental Council of Zambia, where she had taken leave without pay.

I settled back into my teaching position at the University and was appointed lecture Grade 2. This, the second rang of the ladder from the lowest entry point of lecturer 3 in the University academic ranking system. Our daughter Chiku had a difficult time adjusting to the new environment, she began to have very high fevers. We were unable to determine why for a long time. Until one of my friends Dr James Munthali who was a trainee pathologist examined her and found that she had Urinary Tract Infection. This is a common disease of young girls involving the urinary system. She responded very well to treatment, though she lapsed from time to time. However we always gave her empirically the UTI treatment and she always responded well.

I was the first of 5 trainees in Anatomy to return to the University Of Zambia School Of Medicine. Some of the trainees sent earlier had stayed in the United Kingdom. The University and the School were clearly happy they had something to show for this investment. My boss Prof Karashani was pleased about this and put me to work immediately in the Anatomy department. However I was always restless and looking for bigger and greater challenge in my career. It was always clear to me that Anatomy was a programme I had pursued in a quest to be the best Surgeon I could be. My experience in Glasgow had only served to direct me to become an academic surgeon, rather than a simple career surgeon. With these kinds of views I quickly fell out of favour with my superiors in the Anatomy department. When I approached Professor Karashani and subsequently Prof Joseph M Pobee the head of medicine, indicating my desire to do additional training in Surgery, both considered this a sign of dissent and ingratitude. I was hard pressed to find any support from anyone at the time. However I was determined to pursue a more challenging career, and I knew that Anatomy was not sufficiently challenging to satisfy my unbridled ambitions. I had a desire to scale the highest peaks in medicine and to push myself among the greatest and most challenging disciplines in Medicine. My dream was to be a Cardiac Surgeon. So strong was this desire that I was prepared to do whatever was necessary to achieve this goal. The Dean of the school at the time, for a short time was Professor Chifumbe Chintu, he was one of the oldest serving Professors in the school. The head of surgery was Prof Lupando Munkonge. He was much more accepting and moderate in his manner. So I went to see him and explained my ambition. He too made it clear that I could not straddle between the two departments. If you want to be a Surgeon, say so and request for a change of departments, he said to me clearly. This was a completely new approach and one that I felt I had no choice but to take. So I wrote a letter to the Deputy Vice Chancellor Prof Mwenechanya at the time requesting for a change of department.This letter went to the Head of Anatomy,Surgery , the Dean of the school with their comments and finally to the Deputy Vice Chancellor. Fortuitously at the time Prof Munkonge was both Head of Surgery and Dean of the school of Medicine. Prof Karashani had by then made up his mind to allow me to transfer to Surgery and he indicated this. With these comments of support the Deputy Vice Chancellor endorsed my transfer to the department of Surgery. That was only the first of my many battles to achieve my ambitions.

In about February 1995 following several attempts to get better accommodation closer to the Medical school as possible, I had no car at the time. It was becoming a big struggle to get to work at the Medical School in Ridgeway, each morning from Marshlands on Great East Road, the distance being a good 20km. I learnt that one of the expatriate lecturers was resigning and moving to Malawi, he was living in University flats at High rise in Nasser road in Fairveiw.This was a short distance from the Medical School. I quickly applied for this accommodation. We were granted the accommodation by the University and moved in, towards the early part of 1995. It was very convenient, my wife who was working at the Environment Council offices on kabelenga road no more than 10 minutes from Fairview.

Having lived all our married lives thus far in subsidized accommodation we realized that we had no furniture of our own.So when we moved into the Highrise flat number 28 we had nothing by way of furniture. The University was unwilling to loan us neither money nor furniture. The salaries for junior lectures at the time were dismal. We were paid no more than 200 USD dollars per month. It was a big struggle for Theresa and me, to get enough furniture to make the place habitable. We bought a deep freezer on credit, a stove, a bed and some sitting room furniture. The only thing we had which we come with from Scotland was a TV, video and Hi Fi system. I realized immediately the folly of living abroad for too long.

We had saved for a car while in Scotland and out of sheer desperation I had travelled to Dar es Salaam to try and purchase a Japanese recondition vehicle in Tanzania. It was a trip that had proved almost disastrous. I had forgotten how bad the transport system was and I got onto the train at Kapiri with my money on me with the objective of coming back with a car. On the way I developed malaria while on the train which was a 2 day ride from Kapiri to Dar es Salaam(literally the City of Peace). By the time we arrived in Dar es Salaam, I had no peace, I was delirious and paranoid. In the morning some good samaritan helped me locate Mirfin Mpundu an old school friend, who was studying Pharmacy at Muhibili at the University of Dar es Salaam. We got some antimalaria drugs and I was back to normal in a short time. I quickly discovered the cars were much more expensive than I had anticipated, so I returned from a very dangerous escapade with nothing. Following this I decided to order the vehicle from Japan. The process took more than 8 months. In the meantime we struggled with the difficulties of a young family in a big city with no transport. While everybody expected that having just returned from abroad we would have lots of money, it was ironic, but a useful lesson about perceptions. The car came eventually, it was in decent condition, and it was a Nissan bluebird. In those days that was a great car. It helped a great deal to lighten the travel burden.

Having been transferred to surgery, I found that I was now treated as a post graduate student and not a member of staff. I was allocated one of the student shared rooms as an office. Unknown to me I was put on a probationary attachment with Prof John Jellis who was professor of orthopaedic surgery (a specialist dealing with bone diseases). After this I was attached to Prof Mukonge's unit, Red firm. This name had nothing to do with how dangerous it was to work in the unit. The tradition was to name the sections of the Surgery department using common colours. My position was unclear, however under the general care of the Head of Surgery, with some apprehension, my life in the surgical department commenced. It became clear to me that in order to make progress I needed to start surgical training as quickly as possible. Having already passed the part 1 examination of the Royal College of Surgeons of England while I was in Scotland, all I needed was 2 years in a surgical training programme and some money to go to England and complete the final part. This sounded straight forward enough, however it was not as easy to achieve as I discovered to my cost. That supposedly short academic journey would take me, though I did not know it at the time, 7 long years to achieve. My original plan of obtaining a PHD in Anatomy in England, while at the same time finishing my Surgery training, clearly was not going to happen. Therefore given my situation I decided to join the local surgical training programme in the interim, while I looked around for a scholarship. So during this whole period I was preparing for the finals of the Royal College of surgeons examinations. Prudently I applied to join the Master of Medicine in Surgery training programme at University of Zambia. Since I was in the department of Surgery and a member of staff I thought this would be a breeze. It proved much more difficult than I expected. My first difficulty was that the head of postgraduate training happened at the time, to be my former boss the head of Anatomy Prof Karashani. His view was that I was unclear as to what I wanted to do, and was probably taking advantage of the University. He perhaps was correct in this opinion. For almost 1 year I run to and fro between the Head of Surgery, the Assistant Dean Postgraduate (Prof Karashani) and the Director of the Institute of Graduate Studies and Research, who was the head of all postgraduate training in the University. The Director at the time was Prof Lyson Tembo a congenial man as I later learnt. He later became Zambia's ambassador to Japan. When matters appeared to have hit a snag, with some questions about my status in the department of surgery, I appealed to the Director. I was given an appointment to see him. His office which I entered for the first time in 1995 was large and appropriately elegant. His manner was relaxed and he listened to me with great intent. His assessment of my situation was insightful and his logic incisive. He distinguished two things as he put it, admission and sponsorship. The role of the Directorate was to determine my admissibility to the Masters programme, there their responsibility ended. The matters of sponsorship and leave where mine to resolve with the school of Medicine and the relevant University authorities. This little opening given me by the Director was enough for me with determination to get my foot in and to start the Master of Medicine in Surgery programme.

The path was not easy but over the years the school and the University forgot about a nondescript Staff Development Fellow in some obscure part of the University who had changed departments and was doing some local post graduate programme. So I got my acceptance letter from the University into the programme, obtained tuition wavier for my fees and started my training. I was given an exemption from the first year of the programme, in view of the fact that I had the part 1 of the FRCS examinations, which was equivalent to the Master of Medicine year 1. The Master of Medicine training programme is a 4 year programme. It was started at the School of Medicine in 1986; this was 20 years after the undergraduate programme was started. It was structured after the training programmes in England. So it was mostly an apprenticeship training, this meant that student learnt while working under supervision of a specialist, a form of on the job training. While they did this 10% of their time was given to a few choice lectures in the field. During this 4 year period the students sat 2 key examinations and prepared a research thesis which was marked. The examinations were sat in the first years as the part 1 examination, much like the FRCS exams and the part 2 in the final year, much like the part 2 of the FRCS examinations. The only additional thing was the requirement to conduct a written research thesis, which was marked and in surgery an oral examination was conducted. The programme was quite punishing in clinical work load, but being very well motivated it was a punishment I was happy to take. My surgical theory was excellent I found, and my Anatomy training was an added asset. I struggled with acquiring the surgical skills. This was probably because I had spent very little time up to then in actual clinical practice, in fact in surgery itself I had spent no more than 1 month, working as a House Officer, a problem which came to haunt me later when I attempted to register for surgical training in Ireland, with the Irish Medical Council. There was a lot of camaraderie among the trainees and I gradually began to pick up with my surgical skills. By the end of my training in 2000, I had received a number of awards, I was the best graduating student in my class and my research had been awarded the Belgium development price for research in Belgium.

One significant experience was my posting to Monze district hospital in 1996.There was a requirement in the Master of Medicine training programme, for students to spend 6months in an elective district hospital surgical attachment. The objective of which was to become familiar with district surgery and administration of a district hospital facility.The initial objective of this programme having been one of training specialists for this type of facility. Monze is a town in Southern province 180km outside of Lusaka. It is a 3hours drive by road from Lusaka.The hospital is a district Mission hospital which was opened by Bishop James Colby SJ in October 1964. It has almost 300 bed spaces and a catchment area of 800,000 people.The hospital has been run by the Catholic Church for a number of years. There had been an American surgeon there for a number of years called Father Kenneth Johnson. I got to know him quite well later. However by the time I arrived in Monze he had moved to Choma. His replacement was a catholic nun called Sister Ellen Anderson. Monze had also had for many years an Obstetrics programme for post graduate trainees from the University of Zambia. There was a famous Obstetrician and Gynaecologist who was a Catholic nun called Sister O'Brien, she was over 75. She had trained some of the local non skilled classified daily employees (CDEs') to perform operations. She was a well loved Irish catholic nun by the community of the area. During my stay there I worked alongside a number of colleagues who were training in Obsteterics and Gynaecology.The training rotation for our colleagues in Obs & Gyn was only 3 months, while the rotation for the surgical trainees was 6 months. I learnt to speak Tonga, which is the language of the people in the area. I was in Monze from about July 1996 to January 1997. I had the experience of spending one Christmas period there and it proved quite amusing.The single Main Street was filled with people having come from the villages outside Monze. Christmas was the time people came into Monze town and bought goods, especially bread. There was a large Catholic Church in Monze; not very far from the hospital.The hospital is itself, just along the main Lusaka Livingstone road.

My stay in Monze was socially boring. From an academic point of view there was very little to be learnt. From the point of view of clinical skills there was a lot to be learnt. I learnt to perform Caesarian sections and hysterectomies(Removal of the Uterus) in Monze.I must have done over 30 caesarian sections during my stay in Monze.It was about the most common operation done there.The orthopaedic team of surgeons also visited intermittently .

Soon after arriving in Monze, I was amused to be called by Dr Ellen Anderson to her office. She was a 60 something year old catholic nun of the sisters of the Holy Rosary. A typical American she spoke incessantly without pausing. She struck me as a beautiful woman, not withstanding that she was close to 60 and a catholic nun, it was clear that in years gone by she would have been an exceedingly beautiful young woman. She was popularly known as "Kandeke" I learnt later.This meant the plane. This name had to her because of her keen interest in the orthopaedic outreach programme, which was organized by Flyspec, the outreach orthopaedic programme in Zambia under a European Orthopaedic Surgeon. He flew himself on a small B something jet plane up and down the country to perform orthopaedic surgery, particularly among young disabled children, for free.This programme had been running for years in Monze. The rumour was that she was quite taken by this handsome orthopaedic surgeon. I found that she was rather enthusiastic about the orthopaedic visits and appeared to adore the Surgeon.Perhaps this was mere professional admiration which had been taken by the locals for something more.

She took me aside in the week of my arrival for a pep talk, or so I took it. Dr Anderson quickly drew the curtains, which I found amusing, and her explanation even more so. We don't want anyone to think we are doing anything we shouldn't be she said in her highly strung voice. I smiled easily; I considered myself a good student of human nature and was keen to see where she might be going with the pep talk. She did not leave me guessing long. The litany of misdeeds of the local female nurses that followed was instructive if not mostly amusing given that the speaker should be a novice in this type of area. In any case she warned me to steer clear of the nurses. Something I was quite happy to do anyway. She also warned me about some Tonga words that could easily be misunderstood, by the apparently starry eyed young nurses of the hospital. Donot ever say "Muli Baboto" instead of ""Muli Kaboto" the one means you are beautiful and the other how are you, or literally "You are well".I wondered how she had learnt these distinctions herself, given her vocation, and I smiled inwardly. I assured her that I would be on my best behavior and that I was a practicing Christian. She ignored this interjection and pressed her point, perhaps considering that nature was much more potent a force than religion in determining the behavior of a young lonely Doctor among keen young nurses. I packed the advice for what it was worth and kept a careful watch, as I had been warned. To my surprise she appeared less concerned about my surgical skills and experience than she was my social life. I suppose she must have learnt from experience, that students from Lusaka were generally medically competent while being socially inept.

The hospital director was Dr Malama, and the District Director was Dr Mukonka.I knew both from my days at the medical school at Ridgeway campus. The Irish influence on the institution was pervasive as was the catholic influence. The staff appeared heavily regimented and where weary of the constant monitoring and reprimand. This was much the opposite of my experience at the University Teaching Hospital in Lusaka. It was an atmosphere very different from the liberal life we were all used to in Lusaka. The Sisters of Holy Spirit where the congregation that run the hospital, I learnt, they were also called the black sisters.Most of them were Africans. However the Sisters of the Holy Rosary run the hospital in essence, by virtue of their financial influence. They were called the white sisters, most of them were white. I was amused by the politics of religion, which I had been unaware of up to then.

I quickly discovered that Dr Anderson was a hardworking but rather disorganized surgeon. She was also not the easiest person to work with, or be supervised by. However to her credit she was kind hearted, generous and fun to be with on a good day.Dr O'Brien was a much more mature woman.Her surgical skills were highly tuned and some of the best I had ever seen. She had a keen intellect and was extremely perceptive. The two women appeared to get along somewhat uneasily.

The older women giving way graciously to her more impetuous younger friend.I was amused when after working with the one for 5 months, I requested to spend an attachment with Dr O'Brien. My minder was not at all amused. She appeared to take this as a slight on her. Her unhappiness was clear. However since I was determine I pulled it through.My obstetric and gynaelogical rotation in Monze with Dr O'Brien was well worth it. I had not got the opportunity before then to work in OBGYN. I learnt a number of years later that, according to the nurses, that I was one of the few trainees that got on well with Dr Anderson and whom she really liked. This took me by surprise.

Not far from Monze was a congregation of St John of God Brothers, this congregation managed the Holy Rehabilitation Centre for disable children. The group had also run and established the Psychiatric Hospital at Chinama for 50 years, since 1960. They had an insignia at the entrance to the centre written *"Fatebenefratelli"*. Which Dr Anderson let me know was Italian for, literary, "the Do- Good Brothers". My father would have loved that, the do gooders she added generously. I learnt that her father had been rather skeptical about religious faith.We visited this place once a week, to see the progress of various children, and determine any needing surgical operations. The experience was one that would soften the heart of the most hardened of men. The brothers roamed the rural communities of Monze and collected some of the most neglected children with some of the most severe musculoskeletal disabilities I had ever seen in one place. They cared for the children with such tenderness, which I could not have imagined. From that day and since my regard for the practical Christianity of the Catholic Church jumped notches above any other Christian group with which I had associated. These guys were in a league of their own. I did a small study while there to determine the outcome of club foot (an abnormal horse shaped foot) operations in Monze for the last 10 years. We found, though the records were not very good, the success rate for repair under flyspec was over 80%.

While in Monze I learnt a little bit of the local language, Tonga, and I was able to converse reasonably well in it. One of my patients whom, we had treated for a snake bite returned with a generous gift of eggs. I found the Tonga people to be very generous and the language itself not much different from Bemba and Nyanja. I did many operations and improved my surgical skills considerably during my stay.In Obstetrics and Gynaecology in particular; I learnt to do the 3 key operations in the field. These were caesarian sections, ectopic pregnancies (a pregnancy in the tubes instead of the womb) and hysterectomies (removal of the womb).From time to time there was a visiting Professor from Ireland, who came to do Vesical Vaginal Repairs (An abnormal opening between the womb and the urinary system due to a problem during delivery of a baby). I learnt in assisting with these operations, the delicate operations for repairing of vesical vaginal fistulas. This condition results from a delivery that has gone wrong.When a woman goes into labour far away from a hospital, and the baby gets stuck in the birth passage. The process of removing the baby and sometimes the event itself results in damage to the reproductive system and the urinary system. The two systems develop abnormal communication passages. This means the urine or sometimes the stool or both starts coming out through the vagina. The poor young female, as is usually the case becomes a social outcast. She is always wet and smelly. She is soon abandoned by her husband and family.

I had one misfortune while in Monze, when I decided on one weekend to drive my car from Lusaka to Monze. This was a lovely, or so I thought at the time, Nissan bluebird. On my way just outside Mazabuka, the screen was hit by a flying stone, which shattered the windscreen. I was devastated. It took several months to get a windscreen fixed and it cost an arm and a leg. I regretted painful my enthusiasm in driving the car to Monze.

In the last week of my rotation in Monze, I went and picked up Theresa and our daughter Chiku.They spent a week with me in Monze. We visited the nuns at their residence and drove to Livingstone. Dr Anderson and Dr O Brien gave me 100 USD dollars between them. I was very impressed; it was a lot of money back in those days.

We spent a few days at the Hotel Intercontinental then, before it was sold to Sun Hotels. The hotel was right at the Victoria Falls, it was a relaxing and enjoyable time. This was one of the very few times in my career that I have taken time to relax.

From my rotation in Monze I learnt a little more outside the scope of academic surgery. I learnt about life, people and that being successful was more than just being able to practice good medicine. It was about working with different people and making friends. I read this quote in Dr Anderson's office which I have kept to this day. The poem was written by a lawyer Max Ehrmann in 1920. He was a Lawyer from Indiana in the USA.

"Go placidly amid the noise and haste, and remember what peace there may be in silence.

As far as possible, without surrender, be on good terms with all persons. Speak your truth quietly and clearly; and listen to others, even to the dull and the ignorant, they too have their story. Avoid loud and aggressive persons; they are vexations to the spirit.

If you compare yourself with others, you may become vain and bitter; for always there will be greater and lesser persons than yourself. Enjoy your achievements as well as your plans. Keep interested in your own career, however humble; it is a real possession in the changing fortunes of time.

Exercise caution in your business affairs, for the world is full of trickery. But let this not blind you to what virtue there is; many persons strive for high ideals, and everywhere life is full of heroism. Be yourself. Especially, do not feign affection. Neither be cynical about love, for in the face of all aridity and disenchantment it is perennial as the grass.

Take kindly to the counsel of the years, gracefully surrendering the things of youth. Nurture strength of spirit to shield you in sudden misfortune. But do not distress yourself with imaginings. Many fears are born of fatigue and loneliness.

Beyond a wholesome discipline, be gentle with yourself. You are a child of the universe, no less than the trees and the stars; you have a right to be here. And whether or not it is clear to you, no doubt the universe is unfolding as it should.

Therefore be at peace with God, whatever you conceive Him to be, and whatever your labors and aspirations, in the noisy confusion of life, keep peace in your soul.

With all its sham, drudgery and broken dreams, it is still a beautiful world. Be cheerful. Strive to be happy"

I understood that to find happiness was the greatest of all of lifes challenges. That most strive for happiness from external things, that however true happiness, rests in being content with what you have and who you are.

I returned from Monze more skilled both in the art of Medicine and in the art of living. The experience helped me to bear the misfortunes that followed. Within two years of leaving Monze I faced two family tragedies. I think I coped much better because of having worked in Monze. Years later I returned to thank the people of Monze for the steel they had perhaps unknowingly built in my character. When In 2002, I qualified as a specialist in Urology; I returned with a team of trainee urologists and provided urological service once a month for a period of about 3 years. This was my way of saying thanks for the training I got. Many of our colleagues could not believe that we provided this service at completely no charge, except for the cost of accommodation and fuel for our cars which we used between Lusaka and Monze. It was something that I did with great enjoyment.

Soon after my return from Monze, we heard that my father had fallen illness in Mansa, where he had retired in 1988. My elder brother Reynolds, my younger brother Konkola and I drove to Mansa General Hospital. We were informed that he had had a stroke. He was over 60 years old and had moved from the urban life style of a civil servant in town to the rather harsher life of a peasant farmer in his home village in Chipili mission outside Mansa. The stroke had been severe and he had been brought to Mansa Hospital unconscious. I spoke to the Doctors treating him and they indicated that he had been unconscious upon arrival and had made little progress while in hospital. When we got to see him, I was amazed at how much weight he had lost and how sick he appeared. I was not sure that he recognized any of us. He was totally aphasic, that is unable to speak. He was conscious, but had to be moved and feed with difficulty. His sisters who surrounded him were also elderly, clearly outstretched. They were relieved to see us. Mum was still in chipili preparing to join him in Mansa.Mansa Hospital was a provincial hospital, but their capacity to evaluate and manage a disease of this nature was limited. We decided to move him to Lusaka, so we could more closely monitor his condition. The rest of my brothers relied on me to determine whether he was strong enough to be moved by an ordinary vehicle to Lusaka. The distance using the Tuta road, which is the tarred road connecting Luapula province to the Great North road, is a good 800km. We arranged to set up the back of the van which was a Toyota double cab as a bed. I sat with my dad on the long road journey from Mansa to Lusaka. He was clearly the worse off for the journey, but we arrived at the University Teaching Hospital with him in the late afternoons. He was admitted to a Medical side ward in the E11 side ward. We took turns at his bed side and had one of my elder brother's workers spend the night with him in the side ward. He was seen by a team of physicians at UTH, they determined that he had a cerebral vascular accident (a stroke) and he had Cardiomyopathy (weak heart muscle). My dad recovered very slowly but neither recovered his speech nor ever walked again.My mum came from Mansa a few weeks later. When he was better he went and stayed at my elder brother's house in Jesmodine for a number of months. My Dad's younger brother decided that he should be taken to Kitwe for some traditional medical treatment. So eventually he was moved to my other elder brother's place in Ndeke. Where he stayed for a while. However soon after this my elder brother Mulenga Bowa died.He had struggled with respiratory illness for a number of years. He had two children from his first marriage a young boy, Musonda and a girl, Maureen. The news was devastating to my Dad who was still living with them at the time. My wife and I drove down from Lusaka for the funeral.It was a somber affair. The organization he worked for gave the necessary support and he was buried at the local cemetery not far from where he lived in Ndeke. My father stayed in my late brother, Mulenga's house, for a few years until he had a second stroke and died a few years later. The family took the responsibility to take care of the two children that my brother had left.

In 1998 I commenced my research work for my Master of Medicine degree. Among some of the many visiting Surgeons who came to the University Teaching Hospital at the time was a clever British Surgeon called Mr Gregori.In a discussion with him, I got the idea to start some research on the investigation of breast disease using fine needle aspiration method. The technique was simple of low cost and very useful. This gave me a growing interest in Breast Surgery, and I thought I could develop a career in this area. My supervisor was Dr Jim Jewell, an affable Christian missionary who had worked for many years in Luampa mission hospital in Western province.His name summarized his character and that of his wife, for I found them to be precious jewels in their conduct and ability to mentor young sometimes conceited naive doctors like myself. He had decided to retire, but agreed to spend some of his last years in Zambia at the University teaching at the medical school. We became great friends and he proved a great mentor. He had phenomenal surgical skills and could do amazing things in the operating theatre. He was both a general and vascular surgeon. His ten or so years in the rural Zambia as sole surgeon and given him additional skills in tropical surgery which were hard to compare with any. He lived by the most amazing christian principles of generosity, selflessness and service.In the course of my interaction with Dr Jewell I learnt what it was to be a good surgeon as well as a good person. These two things are not necessarily a common combination. In October 1999 I had finished my Master training in general Surgery and took my final written examinations. The University awarded me an overall Grade B in the examination and I was given the award of the Best Master of Medicine (Surgery) post graduate student by the Surgical Society of Zambia.

Soon after this my research work on Fine Needle Aspiration cytology of Breast lumps at the University Teaching Hospital Lusaka was awarded the Belgian Development Prize for Research. This is an annual award given to promising post graduate research in developing countries by the Belgian government. The application needed to be done in both English and French. One of my colleagues on the surgical firm was from Congo and helped me to translate the summary into French. The prize was about 2,000US dollars and included the cost of an Air Ticket to Belgium. Since I had the intention to go back to England to complete the part 2 of the FRCS examinations, I added a little more money and made arrangement to travel from Belgium on to Ireland. I had made an arrangement to do a clinical attachment at the Tallaght Hospital in Dublin. My old class mate and very good friend Elijah Chaila was working at the time in Beaumount Hospital in Dublin as a Registrar in Respiratory Medicine. The arrangement appeared excellent and everything seemed perfect. However I had not accounted for one minor detail that threw a spoke in the works and sploit an almost lovely fairy tale ending.

It was about October 2001 when I flew to Brussels to receive my award. There were about 10 other awardees from different countries. We were received by the Belgian ministry of development. The immigration officials, however, struck me as rather hostile and suspicious. They treated us with some unjustifiable disdain and disrespect. It turned out though, I didn't know it then, but most of us arrived at about the same period. This appeared to have aroused the animosity and perhaps suspicion of the immigration officials at the Brussels airport. We waited unnecessarily long and in spite of having a schegen state visa (the regional country) from the French embassy in Zambia; we were all reissued new visas with very limited periods to stay. This was to be one of my many unpleasant experiences in European cities with immigration officials. This proved to be mild compared to my experience latter in Dublin.

We went to the Belgian Congo Museum in Brussels, who were the sponsors of our trip. The evening ceremony was graced by the Deputy Minister of Culture. The museum had been started by King Leopold and contained several treasures from the Congo. It was a beautiful museum. I suppose it was a way of recompensing Africa for all the abuse of resources to which the continent have been subjected under colonial rule. In any case I found the visit very pleasant. We were very well treated. Brussels as a city was beautiful scenic and very welcoming. We all meet several leading researchers and were given opportunities for further collaborations with research teams in Belgian Universities. I still recall the Professors from the Universities of Gent and Antwerp with their generous offers of collaborations and research visits. I was rather preoccupied with completing my training in surgery with the Royal College of Surgeons at the time and politely avoided commitments of this type. We spent about 5 days in Brussels, with a courtesy tour of the city. We were taken to a tourist spot in the city with a sculpture of a naked boy passing urine "Un garcon puissant" was what it was called. Apparently, so our guide told us, millions of people around the world came to see the statue and throw money into its fountain. Whatever they wished for would come true. So I throw in a coin and wished that I would get a post in Ireland so that I could complete my FRCS examinations. I am not given to superstition, but the events that followed in the subsequent months amazed even me. So I remember fondly my visit to "Un garcon puissant" or more bluntly the pissing boy. I flew to Ireland in September 2001 unsure of what the future would hold. I was hopeful, yet apprehensive.

IRELAND
"THE GAME CHANGER"

Ireland was nothing like I expected. My impression had been, based on my secondary school teacher at Munali Mr Rice. He taught English and always used to say, "You came here for the Nshima, and I know you did not come here for the rice". He was interestingly our English teacher but made a clear distinction that he was Irish and not English. He made all of us believe that the Irish were a pleasant welcoming people, quite the opposite of the English. So I was expectant of a very pleasant stay. I was surprised to find that upon arrival and doing the immigration formalities, which proved somewhat of an ordeal, at Dublin Airport, that I was required to report to the "Guardi" the police within a week of arriving in Ireland, or face arrest, or so I presumed. That was neither the first nor the last of my unexpected experiences in Dublin. I learnt latter, from those who knew better, that my teacher may have been right about the Ireland of yester year. Ten or twenty years earlier Ireland was a struggling backwater of Europe. However by the time I arrived in Ireland, the Irish economy was one of the fastest growing economies in Europe and it was facing an onslaught of immigrants. The authorities were clamping down on this problem with extreme heavy handedness.

When I turned up at the Guardi offices a few days latter, I was amazed at the meandering queque of people, mostly Africans who were waiting to be seen and given permission to continue for a further 3 months in Ireland. It took me about 2 or 3 trips to have my visa extended for 3 months. The immigrants as we were all seen to be were dealt with by policemen in police uniform. The interview process was rather coarse and much of what was required of the interviewee was unreasonable. However this may perhaps had been the result of an excessive pressure of would be immigrants on a small population, unprepared and unhappy to receive so many foreigners all in a short space of a few years. I was relieved to be allowed to stay for 3months and face the Guardi again when my status was better defined.

Dublin was a lot more congested than I had expected, the transport system was well behind the economic boom that was evident in the development of structures and buildings going up all around me. My host in Ireland was Elijah Chaila, he was an old friend of mine from University in Zambia.He and his family had moved to Ireland a few years earlier.He had worked as a general doctor in Chikankata Mission hospital just outside Mazabuka in Zambia for a number of years.He was a excellent Doctor and also had been the smartest guy in my class at Ridgeway Campus. Through his contacts in Chikankata, he had done his post graduate training in Ireland and obtained the prestigious MRCP qualification (Membership of the Royal College of Physicians of Ireland) in about 1996.This was a highly coveted and difficult exam, which was highly respected in the United Kingdom and most of the Commonwealth. So impressed had the Consultant he had worked with in Beaumount Hospital been with his ability, that he had given him an open offer for a job as registrar in his Respiratory Medicine Unit whenever he was able to come back. When I went to Dublin he and his family had returned 2 or 3 years earlier following a brief but difficult stay back in Zambia. He was working as a specialist registrar in Dublin pursuing additional training to become a consultant Respiratory Physician. He had a small family at the time with 2 daughters Denise and Kimberly, who were quite fun to be with. His wife Lydia was an excellent host. I spent 3 months with them in their home in Clondakin in an up market suburb in Dublin. The flat was a modest two storey, 3 bedroomed apartment. My plan had been to complete my surgical training in Ireland and pursue some additional specialist training as well if the opportunities allowed for it.

My attempts to obtain registration for practice as well as commence attachments at the Tallaght Hospital meet with several difficulties. The first of which was that I never got to meet the Professor with whom I had hoped to spend a few months in surgical attachment. Instead I was confronted by his courteous secretary who made it clear that I would only start when my registration formalities with the Irish Medical council were complete. The Irish Medical Council had a list of requirements for foreign trained Doctors wishing to register for practice in Ireland. Among these was a requirement to sit the registration examinations for practice. However before this could be done the Medical documents had to be scrutinized. I duly submitted my documents to the council. A few days later I was surprised to receive the response that my internship period was not suitable for registration in Ireland. It turned out that according to the Irish Medical Council internship period had to consist of 6months in Medicine and 6 months in Surgery. My internship period had been 6months in Medicine and 6months in Obstetrics and Gynaecology. My efforts to convince them that I had spent 4 years subsequently in Surgery and obtained the Masters in Surgery degree yielded nothing. It was a surprising turn of events. It seemed then that my plans to complete my surgical training in Europe had failed. I spent a lot of time feeling dejected and discouraged. During this period I found some books in the Dublin Central Library, where I now was spending a lot of my time, by a church minister called Norman Peale. This was in a section called applied psychology. Nowadays these books are normally shelved under motivational books section.In those days the less appealing title of applied psychology made them a less likely read. Now off courses these types of books have become much more popular and tend to be shelved closer to the entrance of Book shops and Libraries. One of these books, which had the rather unusual title of the "Power of Postive Thinking", struck my eye. Normal Peale I learnt latter had died a few years earlier. He was a Christian minister with experience in counseling and Christian teaching. He was a practicing minister and run his own church in the USA. His manner of writing was very engaging, it was simple yet interesting. The content was much more impressive than the title suggested. So reluctantly and quite skeptical about the value of such information I began to read the book. I think this book quite simply changed my life. Before then my attitude to life had been rather melancholical. My view of life was rather grey and down beat. I had always had a sense of doom or sadness. With always a feeling that life was out to get me and God was plotting my downfall at every turn. I had a premonition that if things could go wrong, they would go wrong on my watch. I had a general feeling of being jinxed, with an unusual dose of bad luck. It was bitterness with life, common I suppose to those who grow up amidst adversity and expect nothing better. Perhaps it had to do with being born on Saturday 13th just missing the ill fated Friday 13th by a whisker. Whatever the case, my expectation of bad luck in life had hanged over my head for as long as I could remember. It was a deposition that made me prone to the most profound level of depression over the smallest misfortune. This habit had only grown more ingrained over the years, as inevitably misfortune comes to all in time.

The book was easy and pleasant to read, it recounted the stories of poor souls like myself and their experiences on applying the positive philosophy thinking proposed by Normal Peale. The ideas appealed to me on two grounds. Firstly it made sense, it made sense because, according to the author the more positive you are about a situation, the more easily you will see opportunities in your environment. The logic of this simple statement was indisputable. If you are preoccupied with failure you will inevitably fail. If you are preoccupied with success you are more likely to see and seize opportunities and succeed. Secondly I had no other option. My situation appeared so desperate I had nothing else to try but a bit of positive thinking. The events that followed my reading the book could only be described as a miracle. Few days after my conversion to the religion of positive thinking, I received a phone call from my wife. She told me that someone from England had been trying to get in touch with me, and needed to talk to me urgently. Somewhat confused about this, I rang the number she had given me. The gentleman on the other side of the line had a perfect British accent. He introduced himself as Mr Peter Belchambers from the British Association of Urological Surgeons (BAUS). The story as it turned out was that I had applied for a scholarship with the International Urological Society(SIU) a few months earlier, which I had forgotten about and was being invited for interviews. Surprisingly as it turned out, these interviews were to take place at the next SIU/BAUS meeting, and get this, in Ireland, Dublin, in the following month of October 2001. Both he and I were surprised that I was in fact already in Dublin. He was more surprised than I was, as it turned out. He informed me that I was one of two candidates selected and the final decision was to be made by the interview panel at the scientific meeting. The other candidate was my friend John Kachimba, who was also a recent graduate from the Master of Surgery programme in Zambia. He was already doing his training in Tanzania at the Kilimanjaro Christian Medical Centre (KCMC) in Urology. I became pretty convinced in spite of my recent conversion to "positive thinking" that my friend was to be given the scholarship. After all he was already on his way doing urology training.

The month moved very slowly, and I shared with Elijah, my feelings that the whole matter would end with John being selected. He tried to reassure me that I stood a good chance, with no success. During this period I spent a lot of time in a park in the centre of Dublin called St Stephens green. It was a serene park with beautiful landscaping of lawns and water fountains. I spent hours looking at people and trying to read their experience of life and their dreams. I saw the young the old, the romantics, the young couples, all sorts of people at all stages of life. It was insightful. On one of these days I run into a twenty something year old Irish guy, he was clearly down and out. He reminded me of the homeless people in Scotland years earlier who would try to sell you a magazine for the homeless called "The big issue"; this was their way of raising money for a meal. What struck me the most was that he was trying to ask me for some food, but could not complete the sentence. His gestures were clearly indicating what he wanted, but the words were gibberish. The Psychiatrist (Doctor of Mental illness) would call it neologisms (fake language). He was making up words which didn't exist. He sat down beside me and we tried to have a conversation without success. I gave him some food, and gathered that he was a drug addict and had been so for many years. The drugs appeared to have so severely impaired his memory and his mind that he was unable to control his own mind. He clearly had severely damaged his Brain function. I was amazed that a man of his age surrounded by the opportunities given to him by birth had so severely squandered them to become so destitute.

The British Urological Association meeting in Dublin was a huge affair, with over 1,000 urologists in attendance. The meetings run over a period of 3 days. John Kachimba had been flown in from Zambia, while I took a taxi from Clondakin, to the up market part of town where the conference was taking place. John and I spent some time attending the scientific meetings which were very interesting. We also spent some time in the city itself admiring the wares that Dublin had on offer. Both Miss Christine Evans , who was a Welsh Urologist, who had spent time visiting Zambia providing urology services, and our mentor Dr Mohammed Labib, who was in charge of post graduate urology training in Zambia were at the meeting. The group that Miss Evans worked with was called Urolink.They provided Urology services to many low and middle income countries in Africa and Asia, where urology specialists were in short supply. I mistakenly thought the scholarship had been arranged by them. Being myself, something of an outsiders to Urology at the time, I felt sure my colleague John, would get the scholarship and I was called up just as a show of fairness. Understanding my chances to be slim I was completely relaxed. A special room was set aside for the interview a little away from the conference hall. I had attended many interviews in the past, however this one must have been one of the most unusual.There were 8 or so people on the interview panel. The president of the SIU at the time Prof Eric Thuroff from Germany, Mr Christopher Woodhouse and Peter Belchambers are some of the ones I recall.The interview run for close to an hour. They took me through a range of questions, from, who I was, to where I had been and what I had studied. The questions were exacting, but I enjoyed the challenge to think clearly and respond concisely. In my recollections on many interviews in the past, I always did well on interviews, but usually I never got selected.

John and I travelled to England as part of the awards and spent some time at the Institute of urology and Nephrology in London. It was a massive structure, with a combination of urology and nephrology at the one site. The director, of this specialist hospital, was the world renowned British Urologist Prof Tony Mundy. He had gained renown in the specialist field of urethral reconstruction (repair of the urine tube). Prof Tony Mundy had a double fellowship in Medicine and Surgery, which was rare in those days and is still so today. He was generally agreed to be eccentric but a genius. The institute attracted people from all over the world who came to train and learn Urology from this world famous center. The Urologist and Surgeon Sir Peter Freyer worked at the institute. Freyer was the first surgeons to remove the prostate (a male organ found below the bladder) through the bladder route, the procedure of transvesical prostatectomy bears his name. Another famous surgeon from the institute was Robert Tanner Warrick. Prof Warrick described and produced a ring retractor for urethral reconstruction which was named after him, the Turner Warrick Retractor. This instrument is in common use even in my urology theatre to this day. His wife Prof Beatrice Turner Warrick became at one time the president of the Royal College of Physicans of England.

During the course of our visit to the Institute of Urology and Nephrology, I was taken aside and told that I had been selected to be the given the scholarship. The title was foundation fellow of the SIU/BJU scholarship. This was the first time the scholarship was being offered and I was to be the first fellow. I was completely taken aback and amazed. The fellowship was to start in March 2002, so I returned to Zambia and spent 6 months in the Urology Unit at the University Teaching Hospital Lusaka, before going back to England in March 2002.

My wife Theresa was 8 months pregnant with our second born daughter, whom we called Lesa e Chumachesu, God is our wealth. In view of my imminent return to England, my wife was induced(artificially delivered) at Monica Chiumyia medical centre in Woodlands on 25th March of 2002.Chesu was a pretty little girl born on the 25th March 2002.Few weeks after I flew to England leaving my wife with our little new born baby.

Theresa, my wife and I, were true soul mates.We fell in love quite by accident without knowing it. We first met at Lusaka Baptist Church, she struck me as petite but very cute. One of the first things I learnt about her was that she spoke her mind. She wasn't over awed by people and had a self assurance that I can only describe as rare. She didn't let anyone put her down and I always felt in the early days of getting to know her, that someone should have labeled her with the sign handle at your own risk. We got along easily though she had a slight sting, when you handled her the wrong way. She was different from other women I had known before. Most women make beauty the centre of the relationship. Their feminity is the glue that holds your attention and most of their conversation is littered with flirtous gestures that keep you on the edge of your seat. Theresa was unusual in this way, she engaged you with her mind, which was a challenge and different. She was agile and followed all my arguments and asked incisive question.It threw me at first! Most women I had know before got impatient with what is abstract and their conversation trialed off to the more mundane things of life, like where did you get that awful looking tie. So for a long time I had always found myself awkward around women. With Theresa, it was different, she had a babyish look that lulled you into a false sense of confidence, but she could certainly punch above her weight. None can really succeed without the help of a good spouse. Theresa has over the years been a wonderful wife. She has always bridled my excesses and moderated my misadventures. When I picked up and went off to England leaving her with a new born baby it wasn't the smartest thing, I have ever done, but she took it with characteristic fortitude.

My stay in England was pleasant but not without difficulties. During that period my father who had become very frail following his stroke a few years earlier died. We mourned him as he would have wanted with dignity and decorum. I was unable to travel from England to Zambia , having just shortly arrived there.

I arrived in England and stayed in a house not too far from the centre of London.The couple had a daughter and were very pleasant. The rooms had been arranged by my sponsors through a group called Doctors in the house.The following day, I went to the Middlesex Hospital which was where the institute of Urology and Nephrology was housed and found no one. It turned out to be a bank holiday.The following day I went back to the British Journal of Urology, which was in Mr Christopher Woodhouses' office. He was the editor of the BJU at the time. The BJU were the managing sponsor for the scholarship. It took a while to settle all the formalities, but by the following week I began my attachment. It was my first experience working in the National Health Services, the British health system. It proved quite an experience. The Middlesex hospital was part of the University College London Hospitals, it was a specialized hospital with over 1,000 beds. Patients there were all urology or nephrology cases. The UCL, had a group of hospitals and just down the street was the main UCL Hospital which had the Accident and Emergency Unit. I was assigned initially to the Unit of Prof Tony Mundy, who was also the Institute Director. He was busy a good deal of the time. His unit was run mainly by a young female Consultant called Miss Tamsin Greenwell. There was an Australian Registrar in our unit as well as a clever nurse specialist. The work was busy and initially my schedule confusing. I was involved in two clinics a week one in Prof Mundys unit and the other with Mr O'Donoghues unit. Mr O' Donoghue had a German trained Registrar who was somewhat overbearing. The Registrar in Prof Mundys unit seemed more preoccupied in getting a grood report and returning to Australia. One interesting practice was the use of the Dictaphones (recoders) after each consultation. Once you reviewed a patient in the clinic you had to also make a written as well as an audio summary of the consultation. I found the practice rather amusing. I held a full time Senior House Officer Job and got a decent pay. This allowed me to move to better accommodation in Belsize Park in North London, a little closer to the hospital. Using the underground train on, what was called, the red line I was at Charring Cross Station within 10 minutes and at the hospital within 5 minutes. We were given pagers when at the hospital, and I recall my pager was 034. I took calls in the hospital every 4th or 5th day. The calls were heavy and involved running between the ageing patients at the Middlesex hospital and walking across to the UCL A&E section of the University of London (UCL) hospital to deal with one or the other urology emergencies. The system of health was more efficient than I had been used to at home, but was also more recriminatory. There was a general sense of caution in dealing with patients; any medical errors were taken very seriously. It surprised me to find that many of the Registrars and Consultant were frequently, unwilling to get directly involved in emergency patient care, probably because of this. If you had a urological emergency in the middle of the night you often had to deal with it on your own. The operating schedules were busy. We had one operating day a week that started in the morning and lasted the whole day. Failure to perform a booked operation was taken very seriously. The hospital would always demand an explanation for a cancelled case. All the hospitals were graded based on waiting lists for clinics and operations. The shorter the waiting list the better the grade and the larger the National Health Service (NHS) grant to the hospital. I learnt quickly that the Urology Institute was a super specialist UK referral hospital and dealt with patients with specialist urology cases. These were patients referred by other urologists up and down the country for super specialist care. The Urologists at the Middlesex hospitals were some of the best in the country; they knew it and made sure we knew it too. This attitude transmitted itself to the Registrars in both Urology and Nephrology. The competition to get an attachment at the hospital was intense; therefore there were people with big egos in the corridors of the Middlesex hospital. I learnt that to get by you had to keep your head low and sit on your ego quite a bit to survive. I worked once a month with a retired Urologist called Mr Milroy, he came in and did parathyroidectomies (removal of a small neck gland) surgery at the hospital once a month. He was a delightful man, with excellent surgical skill. The ability to dissect and even find the small parathyroid glands in the Neck of these patients was extremely delicate work. He was a pleasure to watch. I also worked with the transplant surgeons and assisted in a number of renal transplants; both live donor and non live Donor types. The transplant operations themselves were pretty straight forward, once you got used to the routine.

During this period, I prepared for my final fellowship examinations in Surgery. The Fellowship examination in those days consisted of the basic science part, which was part 1 and the clinical science/surgery part which was part 2. When I was in Scotland 8 years earlier, I had sat and passed the part 1 exams. So, one of my key objectives in getting the scholarship, was to complete the part 2 examinations. I spent a good deal of my free time studying for the examination. The part 2 exams consisted of a written examination, an oral examination and a hospital based clinical examination. You had to pass each step to proceed to the next. I decided to sit my examinations at the Royal College of Surgeons and Physicians of Glasgow. Having lived a while in Glasgow I felt that my best chance for passing was to sit the exams there. My scholarship with the BJU/SIU was short and I figured that I had only one shot at the examination. The training was being changed after the Calman reforms to post graduate training in England. We were told that any trainees, who had not completed their examination, by the end of 2002, would have to start again under the new MRCS system. I was determined to get the qualification before the end of this period. I faced two key problems. The first was getting acceptance into the examination and the second was getting some leave from work to travel to Glasgow for the examinations. These proved less problematic than I had feared. Within 3months of arriving in England, I went down to Scotland and sat the written exams of the Royal College of Surgeons and Physicans of Glasgow. It was an opportunity to visit a town in which I had first been initiated into the United Kingdom. My first surprise was how much the town had modernized and grown. The exam though was in two sections including essays and short notes.It was a decent exams and I faced no peculiar difficulties. There were so many Asian folk I wandered whether I was in England. The exam was in 3 stages each dependant on the performance in the previous one.The written was followed in a week by an oral examination. Invitation to the oral exam was a sign that the performance in the written exams was fair. So when I was invited for the oral exams a week later I was quite pleased. I travelled again to Glasgow by train and spent the night at the fancy hotel by the Cydesdale River a walking distance from the college which was on the St Vincent Street in Glasgow. The place was unnerving as all such places tend to be. We were examined by two sets of examiners in an almost similar manner as was done at the Royal college of Surgeons of England 7years earlier. The two main stations were the principles of surgery and intensive care, and the operative surgery station. Both stations were fair and my performance, by my assessment good. In the operative station, I was asked about how to do a nephrectomy (removal of the kidney).Which was ironic, because that was the bread and butter of a urology trainee. My only self caution was not to be cocky. Some of my friends had warned me that the exam was pegged at the level of a Senior House Officer in England. If you appear to demonstrate too much knowledge in operative surgery this may be weighed against you I was told. So I return to London not unhappy with my performance but still anxious about the results. After a month I got a letter inviting me for clinical examination. This was the last part of the examinations, and indicated that I had reached a passing standard in the exams. My advisers had also said, and I recalled this now, that most overseas students failed the oral basic science part of the examinations, this is because they have more practical than theoretical knowledge. So it was said once you pass the oral examinations, you will pass the clinical examinations. My invitation to sit the clinical examination stated that I would be examined in Elgin, at the Elgin Royal Infirmary. I had never heard of Elgin, so I presumed it to be Edinburgh. Edinburgh is the capital city of Scotland, it's a lovely city, and I was looking forward to the trip. On further examination and searching the web, I found that Elgin was a small town on the east coast of Scotland. My pulse froze when I realized this. I had two concerns. The first was how to get there, the second was, that the accent would be very broad and understanding the examiners would be a nightmare.

Both my assertions proved to be wrong to my delight. I travelled by train to Glasgow and transferred trains to Elgin. The train ride was under one hour. I stayed at a petite little guest house close to the Dr Gray hospital, where the exam where to be held the following day. I took a walk to the hospital so that I knew the route for exam day. The hospital was modest in size and well designed. A little old fashioned and on a rather winding road. When I returned to my room I was reassured by the accent of the workers at the lodge, it was close to the Edinburgh accent.

The following morning I woke early and got myself ready for the exams. There was a waiting room for examinees, in the hospital hall way. I sat surveying the various people coming in and out, looking for potential exam cases and any fellow examinees. When one patient was wheeled through the corridor in a wheel chair my mind was flashing with possible diagnosis, multiple sclerosis, transverse myelitis, spinal trauma and on and on. Experience had taught me that even on a good day, getting a neurology case (patient with a disease of the nervous system), was not a good thing. So a wheelchair bound patient heading to the exam room area was unnerving.

A cheerful looking examiner appeared and asked for me. I accompanied him to the examination bay and he introduced himself and his co examiner. I thing his name was Mr Smith, but memory fails me here.Both their accents where closer to the Edinburgh type accents than Glaswegian, so that eased my nerves. There were two exam bays .In the first they asked me to see 2 patients and in the second two as well. The first two where long cases and the second two short cases. The first was a gentleman who had been admitted with abdominal pain. They asked me to take a brief history, which I did. Being somewhat nervous I wasn't as thorough as I should have been. They lead me through a series of questions, the patient proved to have had Gall Stones, while my mind had fixated on Pancreatitis. It wasn't my best performance. The next case was an incisional hernia, by then I was in my element and breezed through that case. The short cases were a vascular case and a melanoma (Cancer of the skin). Both of which were a cinch. When the examiners where shaking, my hand and telling me to check my result at the college, by the end of the day, I was feeling confident.

By the time I got off the train at Glasgow station, my confidence had waned, I recalled that I had not made the diagnosis in the Gall bladder case and a litany of exams errors dropped my shoulders some. When I arrived at the Royal College Surgeons Offices in St Vincents Street the crowd was a modest one. It was a little before 5 pm, and the results had not been declared. So we waited around uneasily. I took a walk down the high street and returned thirty minutes later. My connecting train was at 7pm, and I was making up my mind whether to leave and get the news by mail. When I entered the College foyer, there was a group around the notice board, I gathered the results had been declared. I held my breath and pushed up among the small crowd to peer onto the notice board. The results were posted by name, and the list was short but included all the student that had been successful at the sitting. My eyes run quickly done the list and to my sheer relief I found my name in the upper column of the list. I was overjoyed and enjoyed the long journey back to London with fond memories of Dr Grays Hospital and Elgin.

Soon after that I finished my attachment at the Middlesex Hospital and prepared to return home.

THE UNZA SCHOOL OF MEDICINE

When I returned to Zambia in about November 2002, I was very optimistic about the future. I had achieved much professionally and academically, or so I thought. I looked forward to a smooth rise in my professional and academic fortunes. This unfortunately did not happen. My first surprise was when I applied for promotion, from the rank of Lecturer grade 1 in surgery to Senior Lecturer and this was denied. I was completely taken by surprise. The head of Surgery then Prof Girashi Desai attempted to console me, but in vain. It was inconceivable to me that a person with my kind of curriculum vitae could be denied promotion. From that time on, I decided to leave the University and get a better paying job anywhere else. So I began some frantic efforts to get alternate jobs, however as fate would have it all doors appeared securely shut. I was invited to a number of interviews. None of which yielded any positive outcome. It was amazing, that being, in my opinion, at the time, one of the most well qualified specialists in Zambia, I was unable to get any other job and leave the University, it was totally unexpected.

I finally decided I should join the armed forces medical corps, I supposed naively that they were short of surgeons and would welcome me with open arms. This proved again to be an inaccurate perception. When I was taken, by a good friend of mine who was as enthusiastic as I was, to the Director Medical Services. We met with an eldery Brigadier General. He made it clear that I would have to overcome several difficult barriers to get an appointment. The list of difficulties he itemized were so long, that I decided right then that the medical corps wasn't the right place. I learnt later that perhaps these encumbrances were exaggerated in order to discourage a young eligible Medical specialist from joining, in order to preserve the careers of many over aged Military Medics, who were being held from retirement, under the pretence of there being no suitable replacements. After this experience, I reluctantly concluded that since I had served in the University for this long, I might as well continue for a few more years till my retirement.

My misfortunes were compounded by some misunderstanding that arose with the University Teaching hospital administration at the time as well. The relationship between the hospital and the University has never been well enunciated, I fell victim to this lack of clarity. The hospital was operated under the Ministry of Health, while the School of Medicine was under the Ministry of Education. The two systems both employed Doctors, one for patient service and the other for teaching. The two sets of Doctors did both. The payments to each of these have been contentious over the years. Suffice to say I got stuck in the midst of this. For some time the hospital administration, withdrew my privilege to practice at the hospital. The matter was resolved but not without some acrimony and some resentment, certainly on my part. So for many years after I provided patient service to the hospital with no pay of any kind at all. None theless I enjoyed my work and grow my experience.

GUEST SCHOLAR

In 2004 the American College of Surgeons awarded me the International Guest Scholar, which is a prestigious international award given to promising young surgeons from outside of the USA. I arrived in the USA in October 2004, it was not unfamiliar to me, because I had travelled there on at least 3 previous occassions. Upon returning from England, as one of only a handful of Urologists in Zambia, I had become involved with the Male Circumcision programme. One of the major health problems that we face in Zambia and Africa, though in a much more diminished magnitude now, is HIV disease. In the quest for solutions to prevent this disease, Male Circumision was just beginning to be advocated as something that may reduce transmission of the disease. When I looked at the scientific evidence, even then, I became convinced of its veracity.

Research data, in 2009 showed this to be true. My involvement in the Zambian programme to promote Male Circumcision for HIV prevention, had allowed me to travel to the United States for a number of scientific meetings.

So I felt pretty confident when I was getting off the American Airlines Flight from Amsterdam, that had taken me from Detroit, Michigan to New Orleans in Louisana.The events of September 2001, had made traveling in the USA by Air a night mare, but I was somewhat used to that experience. They were several checks, you had to have your bags opened and strewn all over the place, while you were left to restore the dignity of your belongings literally on the floor. There where hugh sniffer dogs all over the place with equally hugh Policemen meandering around the endless queques of USA airports. Some dogs would sniff a bag and piss on it and carry on right ahead as though nothing had happened. The meeting of the American College of Surgeon conference was in New Orleans in Louisania, almost exactly one year before hurricane Katrina hit New Orleans.I landed at the New Orleans international Airport at close to midnight. In my misplaced confidence, I had not printed out the Hotel address; instead I had committed the name of the hotel to memory. This proved to be a misjudgement. When I finally got through customs, I was tired jet lagged, and just looking forward to a nice warm bed in a nice cosy hotel. My first surprise was that there were at least 3 hotels of a similar name in New Orleans. I decided to hazard a guess, as I told the cab man confidently, that it was the one closest to the Ernest Morial Covention centre. This proved to be the biggest of the 3 and the most expensive. I have travelled quite a bit in my time, but one of the worst things that can happen to someone after landing in a foreign country, is to find that they have no hotel reservation. This is exactly what happened to me. A costly, 40 minute, cab drive from the airport, I arrived at the hotel. The guy at the reception was tired, but politely did a search of his hotel and the 3 other hotels for various versions of Kasonde Bowa. It was futile; none of the hotels had a reservation under that name. The hotel had some pretty expensive rooms still available and the bill hit the pocket hard enough to hurt. There was no choice, so I paid the bill and promised to check out the following morning.For the price, the room wasnot that great. When my head hit the pillow I didn't stir, I slept like a log.The next time my eyes opened was to the sound of the morning traffic in down town New Orleans.New Orleans had a flavor about it something you could taste, a little salty a little spicy and lots of jive.It was a musical city, the city was where jazz music was born.The New Orleans Airport, where I had landed was called the Louis Armstrong International Airport. The black jazz musican and trumpeter, was born, I learnt, in New Orleans Louisiana.

The following day, I found the hotel where I had been booked and hurriedly moved out.Apparently the whole team of guest scholars had been booked under one name, that of course explained my dilemma of the previous night.

The Ernest L Morial convention centre was a beautiful venue. The centre itself was appropriately clad with the American College of Surgeons regalia, the place was teeming with American surgeons from up and down the United States of all ages. There were conference buses that were bringing attendees from the multiple hotels in the city and the place was filled with activity. The delegates' poured out of the conference buses like runners on a single lane in a city marathon. We poured out of our designated bus and where ushered in to meet the Chairman of the selection committee of the College. The opening ceremony took place in the main conference hall, and we were all directed to sit on the podium with various other recipients of distinction invited by the college. Among these dignatries I meet the President of the Royal college of Surgeons of Glasgow, my own College, Prof Teasdale, we chated and reminisced about Glasgow like old mates.

There were almost 14 Guest Scholars for the class of 2004 that year.I met up with some of the most intellectually gifted Surgeons from all around the world in that group of the class of 2004.In the course of a few days we became fast friends. We moved around New Orleans, together, visiting the old French quarter and the world famous Bourbon street. It was clear the city had a story to tell.

I played speed chess with an old black American guy in the streets of New Orleans, he would pause occassionally, to play the mellowest jazz tune you would ever hear, and then continue to win speed chess against the bemused tourists that poured into the French quarter of New Orleans.

The opening ceremony was a plush event.There was a keynote address, which was followed by presentation of the guests and awards to the scholars. When my name was called I rose to receive the hand of the President of the American College of Surgeons Prof Robert L Laws. I felt that I had come full circle. The surgeons hand carries in it the history of its conquest of the most intricate of diseases, the skill of its achievements over generations, for me this was a meeting of paths. History and destiny are uneasy bed fellows; the one comes while the other goes. When my hand clasped that of the President of the College, I felt a connection of the meeting of history and destiny. It was a big event for me. I felt the compulsion to write the story of my life from then onwards. Throughout my travel in the USA, that year I wrote feverishly, as though the story was dictated to me by a force greater than I.

When the conference was over all, the scholars scattered. They went on, to do their various clinical rotations across the United State. On my part; I had in all 5 states to visit. I was to go to New York, Houston Texas, Cleveland Ohio, Maryland Virginal and California in Los Angeles. I only managed the first 4 states before my money run out. The College had awarded us a fixed student stipend.

I flew from New Orleans to New York, which was my first stop. I was to spend some time at the Sloans Kettering Memorial Hospital in the heart of New York. This is very close to the Trump tower. New York was about as different from New Orleans as one can possibly imagine. While New Orleans had a lingering history about it, New York had a presence and urgency. I had the impression one has with a Microsoft upgrade everything is faster and it has colourful pop ups.The streets were narrow and the buildings were tall, everybody seemed to be going somewhere at break neck speed. You got the impression that if you stopped in the middle of downtown Manhattan you would just get run over by people. Dr Ken Johnson was an old surgical colleague. He is a Jesuit priest from Zambia, who had been at the conference and suggested a Christian guest house for my stay while in New York. The Guest house required a letter of reference to take me in. The rooms were discounted and meant especially for Christian groups. An old Doctor friend of mine from Schereport Louisiana, Tim Nicholls, kindly gave me the reference I required. I stayed in New York for about a week, it was thoroughly stressful, but thoroughly enjoyable. The hospital was a block or 2 away from the New York underground, it took me 15 minutes to get there. The underground train in New York to my surprise was mostly over ground, and was often crowded.

The Sloan's Kettering Memorial hospital was big; the operating rooms were close to 60. The standard number of operating rooms we had back home in Zambia was 8. In England our operating room had 2 theatres. So 60 operating rooms was a maze. There was a TV screen at the entrance to the theatres that listed all the rooms and who were operating where. The individual operating rooms were about as crowded with equipment as they were with people. They were TV screens against each wall in the theatre room. The main operating surgeons had a TV camera on his forehead, which allowed everyone in the room to see what the lead surgeon was seeing at the operating site. For the three or so days I was there, I saw some of the most amazing surgical operations.

It was a pleasure to be in an environment of such amazing human and computer skill. Professor Scardino and his team performed one of the most difficult Urological operations, the nerve sparing radical prostatectomy, with such ease and delicacies I could not hold back my amazement.

My next stop was the MD Anderson Hospital in Houston Texas. The stipend provided by the College for the trip was fast running low, so I decided to travel by train to cut my costs. I got the train from New York Station to Chicago and changed trains' in Chicago for Houston Texas. On our way to Chigaco, we had to de train, and go by road to Syracuse, because of rail track problems along the way on AMTRAK as the train service company was called. We were provided a bus to Syracuse and re trained at Syracuse to Chicago. In Chicago, I got onto the Texas train, which was a double storey train to Houston.

During the course of the journey, I spent a couple of hours at the Chicago train Station, waiting to make my next connection. The old gang star movies we had grown up watching had given me a slightly distorted view of Chicago. Many of these movies had portrayed it as a gangster town, where guys like Al Capone ruled with an iron fist. So inevitably I scanned the Railway Station with suspicion, and the passengers coming on and off the AMTRAK trains with the discerning look of a seasoned police detective. Clearly the trains were used by less affluent Americans, there were groups of Mormons scattered in small groups here and there. I noticed a very obese couple, with an overweight piece of luggage. They were trying unsuccessfully to get it onto the train. Some residual, AL Capone, types discussing in hushed tones across a coffee table. In those few hours I tried to understand and grasp the spirit of the people of Chicago Illinois.

Fortunately it was soon time to board the train and I directed my mind to the more mundane work of writing.

The Texas train was a fun ride. It was a double Decker train, the first I had ever seen. I took a seat on the second floor which gave me a great view of the landscape. America is a large country with vast sways of land across it which is barely habited, I found. Moving from Illinois to Texas, I crossed through states from the central United States to the south east. The train ride was almost 8 hours long. The Texas train, itself should have given me the hint that I was moving from the average to the wealthy. When I arrived at Houston train station, this immediately became clear.

The Oil rich state was as different from New York as New Orleans had been. I had kept my promise to live in the most modest accommodation I could, so I had arranged to stay at a youth hostel close to the MD Anderson Hospital. On the map of the USA the state of Texas, looks like it's giving you the thumbs up sign. Sure enough it should. Unlike any of the other states I had been to thus far Houston, Texas was big in every sense of the word. It had bigger roads, bigger cars and definitely bigger people.The Texans were physical bigger it seemed, they certainly talked more loudly, they also seemed to have bigger hearts. The people of Houston struck me as warm generous and giving. Quite an African trait I thought. So I felt very much at home the few days I spent in Houston. Houston Texas was a wealthy city; it was well layed out and beautifully planned. An Architects paradise it might be said. The city was planned by region, so you had the museums all located in one area, the Shopping Malls and so one. The youth hostels where I stayed for the next five days was modest, more of a house than a hostel.The rooms were clean at the cost, which was about 15US dollars per night.

I visited the MD Anderson Centre the day after my arrival.It was an impressive building with several floors. In Zambia it would have been a fully fledged hospital in its own right.In this case I learnt, it was part of the complex of the Texas Medical Centre, which covered an area over 3000m^2 . It was said to be the largest Medical Centre in the

World, with two Medical schools and 4 nursing schools in the one location. The world famous Baylor College of Medicine was located within the Texas Medical Centre. When I went to the University of Texas Houston for the formalities they asked me about an immigration slip. I told them I had not been given one. This was now 3 weeks ago and none else had asked for it.They made it clear that according to Texan immigration requirements, they could not process my status and therefore my visit. This seemed a bit serious and unexpected. They next day I rummaged through my files and found a small piece of paper cut off, which looked like a receipt for a MacDonalds meal. It really didn't look that important at all. I was amazed, I hadn't thrown it away. The next day, I took it to the admin people and it proved to be the magic wand, which got the wheels turning again.

The MD Anderson centre was basically a specialized centre for the treatment of cancers of all types. The Urology department was specialized as can be imagined in treating cancers of the Urology system. My hosts took me to see the operating room and it was amazing. If the Sloan's Kettering had being large, the MD Anderson OR was humongous. Not only were there more operating rooms but each one was twice the size of the ones I had seen in New York.

One amusing experience I had at the MD Anderson was when a clever young American Urology Professors asked me to watch him do a laparoscopic Nephrectomy, which is the removal of the Kidney using keyhole type of surgery. I had off course never seen this done either in England where I had trained or in Zambia where I worked. So, of course I was very keen.A very exuberant marketing representative had come along to ask the young Professor to test out a new hand device for removal of the kidney.A young resident scrubbed(Special hand washing and dressing in preparation to perform a Surgical operation) in on the case to assist. The operation proved difficult, the young Professor lost his temper and threatened to hit his young assistant with the laparoscope.The market represenrive quickly exited the tense theatre. When the surgeon asked the elderly Professor of Anaesthesia who was keeping the patient asleep, how the patient was doing. The response had us all laughing and eased the tension somewhat.He shot back with the quick response, "the patient is fine, but how is the surgeon". We all laughed. The operation had to be converted to the standard open one and after almost 5 hours the kidney was removed. There was a subway system in Houston that runs through the Texas medical centre; I used it frequently to and from my residence. The drop off station was 5 minutes walk from the hostels where I was staying. The subway station had a shelter which had inspirational quotes from surgeons from Baylor College like the famous vascular surgeon Michael Debakeey.

My next stop was Cleveland Ohio and the Cleveland Clinic. I travelled from Houston again by train to Cleveland Ohio.I timed the trip badly and arrived in Ohio at 12:00 midnight, when I had thought I would arrive at midday. While New Orleans had history, New York had status and Houston had affluence, Cleveland was just a nice ordinary city. It was not much different, I thought, from many of the larger cities one found across Africa. My network of youth hostels had drawn a blank in Cleveland so I was expecting to arrive mid day and have some time to look for reasonable accommodation in the city. I arrived at a few minutes after midnight and I had nowhere to go.The train station was disserted and did not seem like a suitable place to spend the night. There were two cab drivers in the parking lot who offered to take me to one or other hotel for the night. One was a middle aged gentleman and the other a female cab woman of about the same age. After I had agreed to go to the hotel proposed by the cab man and he was happily loading may bags. The female cab woman called me aside and whispered in my ears that the hotel I was being taken too was rather sleazy. I was not sure whether this was a case of sour grapes or not. I took the advise with the candor with which it was given, but having committed myself thus far, I had no alternative, I said thanks and jumped onto the waiting cab. Slightly anxious that I was being taken to a hotel for pimps and peddlers. The hotel was just next to the greyhound station in Cleveland town centre, which increased my apprehension. However it was modestly priced, for a hotel. Compared to my last accommodation in Houston, though, it was expensive. I made sure after I settled in, that the room was securely locked. I was just glad to have found somewhere to sleep for the night. I realized that my travel planning skills needed a serious overhaul.

The next morning I looked around frantically for somewhere a bit cheaper to stay. However, surprisingly, I couldn't find any place cheaper, so against my better judgment I just stayed, and kept the door securely locked each night. There was a DISCO house adjacent to the hotel, and perhaps this was what the lady cab driver had referred too. Other than this I found the place pleasantly non hostile. Some of the guests looked a bit dopey, but perhaps I looked rather dopey to them too. In any case they left me well alone.

The Cleveland clinic was a few minutes from where I stayed. There were no underground or overland trains, I discovered. So I took the bus ride on the main street, which was about 30minutes ride on about the 5th stop to the Cleveland Clinic. The Clinic was, anything but a clinic. It was a large hospital complex. Probably 20 times the size of our hospital back home in Zambia. It was a bit smaller than the Texas Medical centre, but by my standards it was big. Cleverly, unlike the other places, I had been too so far, it blended the hospital service, with hotel and other social amenities imperceptibly well. There was a 5 star Intercontinental hotel in the centre of the hospital, which was linked very nicely into the hospital complex. I learnt that the affluent, mostly Arab elite, often stayed at the hotel, while they were at the clinic. Medical tourism, was I suppose taking hold in the USA as well. I found a lot of this when I travelled to Indian many years later.

My host was the renowned Urologist Dr Andrew Novice, who was the Head of Urology at the Cleveland Clinic at the time. I meet him in his office on my first day at the clinic, and I found him a very friendly and courteous host. I was taken on a tour of the massive facility and observed a number of interesting operations. I observed the famous Urologist Indebhir Gill Singh perform with amazing skill the keyhole (laproscopy) removal of a diseased kidney. I met also a Zambian born resident who was doing his fellowship in laproscopy at the Cleveland clinic.Cleveland was quite a laid back city and I left with very fond memories of my brief stay there.

My next stop was the famous Johns Hopkins University in Baltimore Maryland. This time I had made some efforts to find, or so I thought a suitable guest house using my now extensive network of online youth hostels.Unfortunately , when I arrived it turned out that the hostel had shut down a couple of weeks , earlier for renovations. As fate would have it I arrived again, quite late in the evening in Baltimore Maryland.My travel planning skills, none the better from my experience in Cleveland, or perhaps just down on my luck. In trying to save money I walked from the train station up to the lodge, I am impressive walk of easily 30 minutes.

I sensed something was not right when I found the front door securely locked, and not a soul in site. There were no bustling guests and some of the windows were boarded.I had no cell phone, it was getting late and there was no other guest house within easy reach. I sat down on the steps of the house, prayed and just waited. Surprisingly the Janitor came around on his regular visits to the place, and there I was outside with my suitcase.He was as surprised to see me as I was him. He told me that the place had been closed down for renovations for about a month. I learnt the very humane nature of the Americans in this encounter. Well he said, since you have nowhere to go I'll offer you to stay the night, but there is no furniture at all. This was all I needed, I was appropriately grateful, and offered to pay for a nights accommodation.He refused completely to hear of it. The large reception room was completely bare, he gave me a couple of blankets, and I spent my first night in Baltimore, on the hard cold floor. I was just glad I had found a bed, or was it a floor for the night.I had downgraded from a supposedly sleazy hotel to a defunct guest house.

The following morning, I woke early said my good byes and moved around the neighbourhood in search of a guest house nearby, with no success. The janitor had told me that Baltimore was facing an economic slump.There were few jobs, so very few visitors and hardly any guest houses.My best bet was to go to Washington, which was a 30 minutes train ride from Baltimore. It was clear that this suburb of Baltimore Maryland was in decline there were many derelict buildings, with was hardly a soul to be seen in the streets. I found the local public library and spent some time on the internet looking for accommodation. I discovered an opening at the YMCA youth hostels in Washington DC. Being more relaxed after that I spent some time playing online chess, with some pretty astute chess players. I could not really go to the hospital until my accommodation was sorted, so I got onto the train for Washington DC.

I asked the question in the course of my stay what does the DC after Washington stand for. The explanation I got was interesting. The capital city was the federal headquarters of the USA, and was not to fall under the jurisdiction of any of the states to preserve its neutrality. Therefore a special district was created in Virginia, for the capital city. This was called the District of Columbia, hence the DC.Quite an extraordinary piece of reasoning I thought.

Washington DC had the neat official appearance that capital cities do. It was clearly a city of affluence like Houston, but not openly so.It was busy like New York, but in a modest sort of way.It was ordinary like Cleveland, but in an official sort of way. It had history and flare like New Orleans, but in a guarded sort of way. It had some down and out places, but not immediately obvious like some places in Baltimore Maryland. I liked Washington DC by instinct, it was just like me.Or so, I mislead myself to think.It had an air of discipline and order that made me feel, well pretty safe. I was sure from the time I got off the train that it was the right place to end my last few days in the USA.I stopped for awhile and listened to a black jazz trumpeter come shoe shine man, humming away at a Louis Amstrong tune, and felt I had come full circle in the USA. It was probably time to go home.

I found the YMCA hostels easily and was pleased with what I found.It was secure orderly and clean.It was also reasonably priced. No pimps, peddlers or dopey guests. There were a lot of young people there and I made friends with quite a few. My roommate was a Russian University student who had taken a break from his studies to visit the United States. He claimed his English was poor, but I found it quite good. He was also a pretty clever guy and could give you a good day of insightful conversation. He was pleasant to be with as were many of the other students, most of whom were from eastern European and curious about America. The Washington Hyatt hotel was a block or two away from my hostels, and I thought it would be nice to stroll through the high class world famous hotel and I did. I was not disappointed. Being a connoisseur of Hotels, I promised myself to spend a night one day at one of the Hyatt Hotels, and I did, but that's another story

Having grown up as I did in a place of scarcity, I had developed affection for vanity. I therefore always aspired for association with great things, great places and great people. Johns Hopkins Hospital was a great place. When I came to the USA, I was unaware of all the other magnificent hospitals I had thus far visited, but I had been aware for many years of the Johns Hopkins Hospital in Baltimore Maryland. It was the price jewel in my collection and appropriately the last one on my list. So, I was excited to visit for the first time the Johns Hopkins University Hospital. The operating rooms were much like what I had seen in New York, Houston and Cleveland. The surgeons were perhaps more famous, and there were a lot more visiting physicians life me. I watched Prof Parthin, who was a world renowned Urologist performs the removal of the prostate gland, an operation called a radical prostatectomy, and I had the feeling of being in heaven. So pleased was I with my stay, I decided to spend my last few days in the USA, visiting the famous sites of Washington DC. My many young room mates who were primarily touring the USA, were very keen to give me the list of places to go, it was an inexhaustible list. I choose about 4 of these and spend my last few days in the USA among the tourists.

Arlington Cemetery, which is a little outside Washington DC, was my first tourist stop. It was where John F Kennedy was buried. I caught a train ride, and arrived at a vast elegant cemetery. Well arranged rows of white tomb stones, made the site scenically beautiful. It was a sprawling large graveyard in which all the distinguished American leaders and many of the American soldiers were buried. The history of American lay in this vast grave site. It is, in Arlington, Virginia, just across the Potomac River and the Lincoln memorial. The boundaries between Washington DC, and Arlington, were imperceptible to me and probably also to many other equally naïve tourists.

We were told the site is over 253 hectares and has over 400,000 graves. It took a full day to tour the site. On John F Kennedys' grave there was a plaque with a continual burning flame in the centre. The experience was moving.

My next stop was the Okinawa statue. This is located in the heart of Washington DC. It is said by those wiser than I, that if you want to know a people go to their burial ground and their hospitals. It tells you how they treat the most vulnerable and the weakest people in their communities. This will tell you the character of their hearts. So I had seen the hospitals and now I was seeing the grave sites. The hospitals were impressive and I found the grave sites equally so. Okinawa statue was of 4 USA marines hoisting the USA flag after the battle of Okinawa on the Japanese Island in 1945. There was a very insightful quotation on the side of the monument with the words, "When uncommon valor was a common virtue". The English was old, but the meaning was fresh, in plain English, it said, when great courage was common.

The Lincoln Memorial was in a category of its own. It was a package, with the statue of Abraham Lincoln in this mausoleum, the reflecting pool, the Vietnam Wall Memorial and the Washington Memorial. Incidentally, I noted with pride, that Abraham Lincoln was born on the 12th February, 1809 a day shy of my own birth day. This, a reminder of the vanity born from scarcity, I had mentioned earlier. This Lincoln Memorial was where Martin Luther King had made his famous I have a dream speech. Some years later Barrack Obama, the first black American President was inaugurated at the site.

I remember watching in grade 5 in my primary school, in Kitwe in Zambia. The moving speech of Martin Luther King junior.Its was a speech many of us had memorized at the time.Together with this a close friend of mine at the time Katai Nkhata, had memorized the full Gettysburg address, which Lincoln gave after the battle at Gettysburg. This speech is inscribed on the wall in the Lincoln Memorial. The Vietnam wall memorial was just next to the Lincoln Memorial.

The White House on 1600 Pennsylvania Avenue was the last place I visited. It was a lot bigger than what it appears in movies. The place was teeming with tourists. The house has many faces which take a while to get round. The perimeter fence is quite wide and the House is only seen at a bit of a distance. I walked right round it and got a very nice view of it. In contrast to Buckingham Palace in the UK, where tourists actually get to go into the place, the White house was more restricted, and probably justifiably so. I spent some time at the Martin Luther King library in the centre of Washington DC, and enjoyed my final days in the USA just visiting places of interest.

I had travelled through the USA with that heavy sense of destiny and purpose for almost 4 weeks. I visited some of the top Urology training institutions in the USA. I went to the Sloan's Kettering Memorial Hospital in New York, the MD Anderson Hospital in Houston Texas, the Cleveland Clinic in Cleveland Ohio and the Johns Hopkins Hospital in Baltimore Maryland. I also met some of the top American Urologists including Dr Andrew Novick, Dr Peter Scardino and Dr Patrick Walsh.I travelled mostly on the east coast of the USA. I travelled a great deal by train, because the stipend provided was small. It allowed me to become more intimate with the country itself and it's people. I stayed in modest accommodation, youth hostels and bread and breakfast places. It surprised me to find that the American people were kind and generous. It also surprised me to find that many America people are poor and illiterate.

I returned home, the richer for my experience. My sense of mission and purpose was invigorated. Unknown to me at the time, I was to become several years later the First Dean of the second public Medical

School in Zambia and the first Zambian professor of Urology, but that's another story maybe for another author.

Glossary

(The meaning of difficult words)

Word	Meaning	Word	Meaning
1. Abandoned 2. Accentuate 3. Accomplished 4. Adversaries 5. Affable 6. Ailment 7. Aisle	Left alone Add on top of Skilled Opponents Pleasant Illness Passage	14. Austere 15. Averse 16. Avid 17. Baited 18. Banter 19. Besiege 20. Benefactor	Severe Against Enthusiastic Anxious Small talk Surround Supporter
8. Animist 9. Arrogant 10. Assertive 11. Astute 12. Authoritarian 13. Autobiographical	Belief in spirits Proud Pushy Clever Strict A story someone writes about his own life	21. Bland 22. Brawn 23. Brush 24. Bureaucratic 25. Bustling 26. Caliber 27. Candid 28. Camarederie 29. Changrin	Plain Labour/Work Impatient Follows rules Busy Quality Frank Friendliness Sadness

Word	Meaning	Word	Meaning
30. Circuitous	In a round about way	47. Designated	Allocated
31. Clarion call	A call to arms	48. Detractors	Enemies
32. Clinician	Hospital worker	49. Dexterity	Skill
33. Coarse	Rough	50. Dialect	Minor Language
34. Conceited	Proud	51. Dichotomy	Two paths
35. Conceivable	Possible	52. Dignity	Respect
36. Conscientious	Careful	53. Digs	Rooms
		54. Dilapidated	Untidy
37. Consummate	Skilled	55. Disarmingly	Charming
38. Contemplated	Think well	56. Disclaimer	Excuse
39. Cosmopolitan	Of a city	57. Disenchanted.	Unhappy
40. Cowered	Frightened	58. Disharmony	Disagreement
41. Cynicism	Doubt	59. Disheartening	Saddening
42. Decent	OK	60. Disheveled	Untidy
43. Demean	Bring down	61. Dispute	Argue
44. Demeanour	Conduct	62. Dissipate	Release
45. Demise	Death	63. Dominance	Control
46. Demure	Small	64. Dope	Fool
47. Delusion	Mistaken belief	65. Dubious	Doubtful
48. Desecrate	Make unholy	66. Elated	Happy

Word	Meaning	Word	Meaning
67. Elitist	For upper classes	90. Hub	Centre
68. Elusive	Special	91. Impassioned	With passion
69. Embed	Hidden within	92. Impending	About to occur
70. Eminence	Prominence	93. Inadvertently	Accidently
71. Encyclopedic	Vast	94. Incisive	Accurate
72. Equity	Equal	95. Indifferent	Little interest
73. Erratic	Unreliable	96. Indigenous	Local
74. Extolled	Regarded highly	97. Indolent	Laid-back
75. Exuberance	Full of life	98. Innocuous	Innocent
76. Foray	A short journey	99. Intellectual	Intelligent
77. Fortitude	Strength	100. Interred	Imprisoned
78. Fragment	Break down	101. Intriguing	Strange
79. Frustration	Disappointment		
80. Futile	Bearing no fruit	102. Introvert	Withdrawn
81. Geriatrics	Disease of the Elderly	103. Intrusion	Invade
82. Gender	Sex	104. Ironic	Funny
83. Genu Flex	Kneeling	105. Knack	
84. Glean	Pick up	106. Lanky	Tall
85. Gloom	Sadness	107. Leaning	Resting
86. Grit	Inner Strength	108. Legend	Hero
87. Grovel	Beg	109. Linger	Hang around
88. Hard pressed	Under pressure	110. Linguistic	Languages
89. Hirtherto	From here on	111. Literacy	Reading

Word	Meaning	Word	Meaning
112. Livid 113. Lumbered	Annoyed Burdened	135. Pediatrics 136. Peers	Diseases of Children Friends
114. Medicine 115. Mirth	Study of Disease Laughter	137. Perception 138. Pessimism	Belief Doubt
116. Mischievous 117. Modest	Naughty Humble	139. Petite 140. PHD	Small Research Degree
118. Mundane 119. Myriad	Routine Many	141. Physician 142. Plenary	Doctor Combined
120. Naive 121. Native	Lacking experience Local	143. Prestigious 144. Proficient	Respected Skillful
122. Novice 123. Oblivious 124. OBS & GYN	New Unaware of Obstetrics and Gynaecology	145. Purgatory 146. Queer	Awaiting Heaven Unusual
125. Obscure 126. Obstetrics	Unimportant Field of Medicine dealing with child birth	147. Reckless Enthusiasm 148. Recluse	Overly excited Withdrawn
127. Of means 128. Onerous	Rich Making some tired	149. Reconcile 150. Relish	Bring together Like
129. Ophthalmology 130. Organist	Eye specialist Church pianist	151. Renown 152. Reticence	Famous Reserved
131. Otorhinolaryngology 132. Panache & Finesse	Diseases of the Ear, Nose and throat With excellence	153. Revert 154. Rigour	Go back to Energy
133. Paralyzed 134. Patronage	Unable to walk Favouritism	155. Royalty 156. Savvy	Like a King Street wise

Word	Meaning	Word	Meaning
157. Scamper 158. Skepticism	Run away Doubt	178. Valor 179. Verbose	Courage Talkative
159. Somber 160. Spluttered	Serious Spill all over	180. Villain 181. Volatile	Crook Bad Tempered
161. Spurious 162. Stethoscope	Weak Doctors instrument to listen to the heart	182. Vulnerabilities	Weaknesses
163. Stigmatized 164. Stilted	Label Abnormal		
165. Studious 166. Subordinate	Some who reads a lot Below another		
167. Superstition 168. Surgery 169. Tantrum	Belief in the supernatural Branch of medicine dealing with operations Episodes of Hot temperedness		
170. Trepidation 171. Trivial	Fear Small		
172. Tyrannical 173. Ultimate	Role with force Final		
174. Unit 175. Unyielding	Team Not bending		
176. Vacillate 177. Validity	Chancing The proof of		

PHOTO ALBUM

Family picture in 1970 at Kulumba Photo Studio in Mansa Mum and Dad, Konkola, Chanda and Mulenga. I am the middle boy pointing at the camera.

In Mansa 1970 with my four brothers. Outside our house in Kobaniya. I am the boy in front on the tricycle. In the background my Dads Zefa vehicle.

Meeting with 1st President Dr Kenneth Kaunda at State House 1988

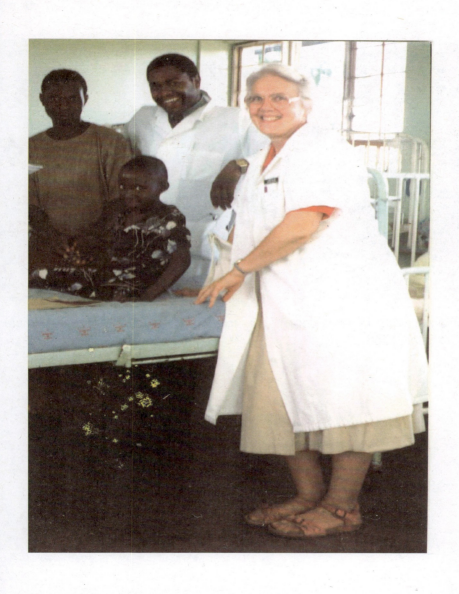

With Dr Ellen Anderson at Monze Hospital in 1996

Meeting with 1st President of Zambia Dr K D Kaunda as a medical student in 1988

Grandfather Mr. Basil Bowa in Chipili Mission

MBChB graduation in 1990 with James Chipeta and Gershom Singogo

Graduating on the post graduate M.Med degree as best student in Surgery

With Dr Jim Jewell and Dr P Tembo

With Theresa at Eric Sinyangwes wedding in 1989 and Jacob Toka

As the page boy

CBU graduation ceremony 20th June 2011 as the Founding Dean of the CBU School of Medicine.

As Vice President of the Zambia Medical Association 2005,with Standing L-R Dr F Goma now Dean UNZA SOM,Dr Peter Mwaba now Permanent Secretary,Prof K S Baboo,Dr Francis Kasolo WHO Afro, Dr P Njobvu Now Brigadier General Commandant Maina Soko Military Hospital.Seated L-R Dr Rosemary Kumwenda UNDP and Dr Mary M Zulu now Registrar Health Professions Council of Zambia.